*The Seagull Sartre Library*

*The Seagull Sartre Library*

*The Seagull Sartre Library*

VOLUME 9

# OCCASIONAL PHILOSOPHICAL WRITINGS

**JEAN-PAUL SARTRE**

TRANSLATED BY
CHRIS TURNER

LONDON NEW YORK CALCUTTA

EXCLUSIVELY DISTRIBUTED IN INDIA BY
**Atlantic Publishers and Distributors (P) Limited**
7/22 Ansari Road, Darya Ganj, New Delhi
**www.atlanticbooks.com**

This work is published with the support of
Institut français en Inde – Embassy of France in India

Seagull Books, 2021

Originally published in Jean-Paul Sartre,
*Situations I* © Éditions Gallimard, Paris, 1947

These essays were first published in English translation
by Seagull Books in *Critical Essays* (2010)
English translation © Chris Turner, 2010

ISBN 978 0 8574 2 912 4

**British Library Cataloguing-in-Publication Data**
A catalogue record for this book is available
from the British Library

Typeset by Seagull Books, Calcutta, India
Printed and bound in India by Atlantic Print Services

# CONTENTS

※

## CARTESIAN FREEDOM

Freedom is indivisible, but it manifests itself in different ways, depending on circumstances. To all the philosophers who set themselves up as its defenders, we may ask a preliminary question: in respect of what special *situation* have you experienced your freedom? It is one thing to feel you are free in the realm of action, of social or political activity or of creation in the arts, and another to experience it in the act of understanding and discovering. A Richelieu, a Vincent de Paul or a Corneille would have had some things to say about freedom, had they been metaphysicians, because they seized it from the one end, at a point when it manifested itself through an absolute event, through the appearance of something new, whether a poem or an institution, in a world that neither called for nor rejected it. Descartes, who is a metaphysician first and foremost, comes at matters from the other end: his primary experience wasn't one of creative freedom *ex nihilo*, but of autonomous thought which, by its own power, discovers intelligible relationships between existing essences. This is why we Frenchmen, who have been living by Cartesian freedom for three centuries, implicitly understand 'free will' as the practice of independent thought rather than the production of a creative act, and, like Alain, our philosophers in the end equate freedom with the act of judging.

This is because, in the thrill of understanding, there is always the joy of feeling ourselves responsible for the truths we discover. Whoever the master may be, a moment comes when the disciple faces the mathematical problem all on his own; if he doesn't bring his mind to grasp the relationships, if he doesn't himself produce the conjectures and schemas which apply just like a grid to the figure in question and will reveal its principal structures and if he doesn't, lastly, bring about a decisive insight, then the words remain dead signs and everything is merely learned by rote. In this way, if I examine myself, I can feel that intellection isn't the mechanical outcome of a pedagogic procedure, but originates solely in my will to lend attention, in my exertion alone, in my refusal to be distracted or to hurry and, ultimately, in the whole of my mind, to the radical exclusion of all external actors. And this is precisely Descartes's initial intuition: he understood better than anyone that the tiniest move in thought involves the whole of thought, an autonomous thought that posits itself, in each of its acts, in its full and absolute independence.

But, as we have seen, this experience of *autonomy* doesn't coincide with the experience of *productivity*. This is because thought has to have *something* to understand, objective relationships between essences, structures, a sequence: in short, a pre-established order of relationships. Thus, as the price to be paid for freedom of intellection, the path to be travelled is as rigorous as can be:

> Since there is only one truth in any matter, whoever discovers it knows as much about it as can be known. For instance, a child who has been taught arithmetic and does an addition according to the rules may be assured that he has discovered all that the human mind can discover as regards the sum he is considering. Indeed, the method of following the proper order and exactly enumerating all conditions of the problem comprises everything that gives the rules of arithmetic their certainty.[1]

Everything is established in advance: the object to be discovered and the method. The child who applies his freedom to doing an addition sum by the rules

---

1 René Descartes, 'Discourse on the Method', Part II, in *Philosophical Writings* (Elizabeth Anscombe and Peter Thomas Geach trans.) (London: Nelson's/The Open University, 1970), p. 22 (translation modified).

doesn't enrich the universe with a new truth; he merely recommences an operation that a thousand others have performed before him and that he will never be able to take farther than they have. The attitude of the mathematician is, then, a rather striking paradox and his mind might be said to be like that of a man who, having set off down a very narrow path, where each of his steps and the very posture of his body were rigorously conditioned by the nature of the ground and the necessities of the walking, was imbued, nonetheless, with the unshakable conviction that he was accomplishing all these acts freely. In short, if we start out from mathematical intellection, how shall we reconcile the fixed, necessary nature of essences with freedom of judgement? The problem is even more difficult, given that, in Descartes's day, the order of mathematical truths was regarded by all right-thinking people as a product of divine will. And since there was no way round that order, Spinoza preferred to sacrifice human subjectivity to it: he would show truth developing and asserting itself under its own impulsion *through* those incomplete individualities that are the finite modes. Faced with the order of essences, subjectivity can only be the mere freedom to adhere to the truth (the way certain moral philosophers argue that one's only *right* is to do one's *duty*) or else it is confused thinking, a mutilated truth, the subjective character of which can be dispelled by development and clarification. In the latter case, man disappears and no difference remains between thought and truth: the true is the totality of the system of ideas. If one wants to rescue man, all that remains—since he cannot *produce* any ideas, but merely contemplate them—is to endow him with a simple negative power, the power to say 'no' to everything that isn't the truth. And so, in the guise of a unitary doctrine, we find two rather different theories of freedom in Descartes, depending on whether he is looking at his power to understand and to judge or simply wishing to rescue man's autonomy in its confrontation with the rigorous system of ideas.

His spontaneous reaction is to assert man's responsibility towards the truth. Truth is a human affair, since I must affirm it for it to exist. Before I pass *judgement*, which is the adherence of my will and a free commitment of my being, there exist only neutral, floating ideas that are neither true nor false. Hence man is the creature through whom truth appears in the world: his task is to commit himself totally, so that the natural order of existents may become an order of truths. He must think the world, will his thought, and transform the order of being into a system of ideas. In this, from the *Meditations* onwards, he emerges as that 'ontico-ontological' being of which Heidegger will later speak. Descartes begins, then, by bestowing total intellectual responsibility upon us. Every moment, he feels the freedom of his thought in regard to the sequence of essences. And he feels his loneliness too. Heidegger has said, No one can die for me. But before him, Descartes said, No one can understand for me. In the end, you have to say yes or no—and decide what is true, alone and for the entire universe. Now, this adherence is a metaphysical, absolute act. Commitment isn't relative; we aren't speaking of an approximation that can be revisited. But just as, for Kant, the moral individual acts as legislator of the community of ends, Descartes, as scientist, decides on the laws of the world, for the 'yes' that one has eventually to pronounce before the reign of truth can come about demands the commitment of an infinite power that is given all at once: there is no way of saying 'slightly' yes or 'slightly' no. And man's 'yes' is no different from God's:

> It is only the will, or freedom of choice, which I experience within me to be so great that the idea of any greater faculty is beyond my grasp; so much so that it is above all in virtue of the will that I understand myself to bear in some way the image and likeness of God. For although God's will is incomparably greater than mine, both in virtue of the knowledge and power that accompany it and make it more firm and efficacious, and also in virtue of its object, . . . nevertheless it does not seem any greater than mine when considered as will in the essential and strict sense.[2]

---

2 René Descartes, 'Fourth Meditation', in *Meditations on First Philosophy* (John Cottingham ed. and trans.) (Cambridge: Cambridge University Press, 1996), p. 40.

This complete freedom, precisely because it isn't a matter of degrees, clearly belongs equally to every human being. Or rather—since freedom isn't a quality among others—it is clear that every human being *is* freedom. And the famous assertion that good sense is the most widely shared thing in the world doesn't simply mean that every man has in his mind the same germs of thought, the same innate ideas, but 'goes to show that the power of judging well and distinguishing truth from falsehood, is naturally equal in all men.'[3]

A human being cannot be more of a human being than others, because freedom is similarly infinite in each one. In this sense, no one has shown the link between the spirit of science and that of democracy better than Descartes, since universal suffrage couldn't be based on anything other than this universal capacity for saying yes or no. And we can, no doubt, find many differences between human beings: one will have a sharper memory, another a broader imagination; one will grasp things more quickly and another will compass a wider field of truth. But these qualities aren't constitutive of the notion of Man: we have to see them simply as chance bodily attributes. And what alone characterizes us as human creatures is the use we freely make of these gifts. It matters little how quickly we have understood, since understanding, however it comes to us, must be total for

3 Descartes, 'Discourse on the Method', Part I, in *Philosophical Writings*, p. 7.

everyone or not exist at all. If Alcibiades and the slave understand the same truth, then they are entirely alike in understanding it. Similarly, a man's situation and powers cannot increase or limit his freedom. Here, following the Stoics, Descartes made a crucial distinction between freedom and power. To be free isn't, in any way, to be able to do what one wishes, but to wish to do what one is able to:

> There is nothing that is entirely within our power except our thoughts; this is, at least, the case if one takes the word 'thought' as I do for all the operations of the soul, so that not only meditation and willing, but even the functions of seeing, hearing, determining to perform one movement rather than another etc., inasmuch as they depend on it, are thoughts . . . I did not mean by this that external things are not at all in our power, but only that they are so insofar as they may follow from our thoughts, and not *absolutely* or *entirely*, because there are other powers outside of ourselves which can prevent the effects of our intentions.[4]

Thus, with variable and limited power, man has total freedom. We glimpse here the *negative* aspect of freedom. For, ultimately, if I do not have the power for a particular

---

4 René Descartes, 'A***' (March 1638), in *Oeuvres et lettres* (Paris: Gallimard/NRF, 1953), pp. 1001–02.

action, I must abstain from desiring to perform it: 'to try always to conquer myself rather than fortune; to change my desires rather than the order of the world'.[5] In short, to practise *epoche* in the field of morality. Freedom, nevertheless, in this initial conception, has a certain 'efficacity'. It is a positive, constructive freedom. It probably cannot change the quality of the movement that is in the world, but it can modify the direction of that movement:

> The soul has its principal seat in the little gland in the middle of the brain, whence it radiates into all the rest of the body by the mediation of spirits, nerves, and even blood . . . And the whole action of the soul consists in this: merely by willing something, it makes the little gland to which it is closely joined move in the way required to produce the effect corresponding to this volition.[6]

It is this 'efficacity', this constructiveness of human freedom that we find at the origin of the *Discourse on the Method*. For, ultimately, the Method is *invented*: '[C]ertain paths that I have happened to follow ever since my youth have led me to considerations and maxims out of

---

5 Descartes, 'Discourse on the Method', Part III, in *Philosophical Writings*, p. 26.

6 René Descartes, *The Passions of the Soul* (Stephen H. Voss trans.) (Indianapolis: Hackett Publishing Company, 1989), pp. 37, 41.

which I have *formed* a method . . .'[7] Better still, each rule
of the Method (except the first) is a maxim of action
or invention. Doesn't the analysis prescribed by the
second rule call for a free and creative judgement that
produces schemas and conceives hypothetical divisions
that it will verify shortly afterwards? And mustn't the
order advocated in the third rule be sought and prefig-
ured amid disorder before one submits to it? The proof
is that if it doesn't actually exist, it will be invented:
'establishing an order in thought even when the objects
had no natural priority one to another'.[8] And don't the
enumerations of the fourth precept presuppose a power
of generalization and classification specific to the human
mind? In a word, the rules of the Method are on the level
of Kantian schematism; they represent, all in all, very
general directives for free, creative judgement. And
wasn't Descartes the first, while Bacon was teaching the
English to follow experimental findings, to call on physi-
cists to precede their experiments with hypotheses? In
this way, we discover first in his works a magnificent
humanistic affirmation of creative freedom, which constructs the truth one piece at a time; which at every
moment anticipates and prefigures the real relations
between essences by producing hypotheses and schemas;

---

7 René Descartes, 'Discourse on the Method', Part I, in *Philosophical
Writings*, p. 8. The emphasis is Sartre's. [Trans.]

8 Descartes, 'Discourse on the Method', Part I, in *Philosophical
Writings*, p. 21.

which—equal for God and for man, equal in all men, absolute and infinite—forces us to assume that fearful task that is supremely *ours*: to cause a truth to exist in the world, to make the world true; and which disposes us to live with *generosity*, 'a sentiment that everyone has of his own free will, combined with the resolve never to be lacking in it'.

But the pre-established order intervenes here immediately. For a philosopher like Kant, the human mind constitutes truth; for Descartes, it merely discovers it, since God has established all the relationships that pertain between essences once and for all. Moreover, whatever path the mathematician has chosen to solve his problem, he cannot doubt the result once it has been arrived at. The man of action, contemplating his undertaking, can say: this is mine. But not the man of science. As soon as he discovers it, the truth becomes foreign to him: it belongs to everyone and to no one. He can merely register it and, if he sees the relations that make it up clearly, he doesn't even have the scope to doubt it: seized by an inner illumination that drives his entire being onward, he can only lend his adherence to the theorem that has been discovered and, hence, to the order of the world. The judgements '2 and 2 make 4' or 'I think, therefore I am' are of value only insofar as I affirm them, but I cannot help but affirm them. If I say that I don't exist, I am not even creating a fiction; I am simply bringing together words whose meanings destroy each other, just as they would if I spoke of square circles or three-sided cubes. The Cartesian will is forced into affirmation:

> For example, during these past few days I have been asking whether anything in the world exists, and I have realized that from the very fact of my raising this question it follows quite evidently that I exist. I could not but judge that something which I understood so clearly was true; but this was not because I was compelled so to judge by any external force, but because a great light in the intellect was followed by a great inclination in the will . . .[9]

Descartes clearly persists in terming this irresistible adherence to what is obviously the case 'free', but this is because he lends a totally different sense to the word 'freedom' here. Adherence is free because it isn't given under any constraint external to ourselves; in other words, it isn't caused by a movement of the body or by psychological impulsion: we are not on the terrain of the passions of the soul. But if the *soul* remains independent of the body in the process of assenting to evidence, and if, in terms of the definitions in the *Treatise on the Passions*, we may call the affirmation of clearly and distinctly conceived relations an action of the thinking substance taken in its totality, then if we consider the will

9 Descartes, 'Fourth Meditation', in *Meditations on First Philosophy*, p. 41.

in relation to the understanding, these terms no longer have any meaning. For a moment ago we termed the possibility for the will itself to determine whether it said 'yes' or 'no' to the ideas conceived by the understanding 'freedom'; this meant, to put it another way, that the die was never cast, the future never predictable. Whereas now, with regard to cases of obvious fact, the relation of the understanding to the will is conceived as a rigorous law, in which the clarity and distinctness of the idea play the role of determining factor where affirmation is concerned. In short, Descartes is much closer here to Spinoza and Leibniz, who define the freedom of a being by the development of its essence independently of any external action, although the moments of that development follow one upon the other with rigorous necessity. It is at this point that he goes so far as to deny the freedom of 'indifference' or, rather, to make it the lowest degree of freedom:

> For in order to be free, there is no need for me to be capable of going in each of two directions [*indifférent*]; on the contrary, the more I incline in one direction—either because I clearly understand that reasons of truth and goodness point that way, or because of a divinely produced disposition of my inmost thoughts—the freer is my choice.[10]

10 Descartes, 'Fourth Meditation', in *Meditations on First Philosophy*, p. 40 (translation modified).

The second term of the alternative—'because of a divinely produced disposition of my inmost thoughts'—concerns faith in the strict sense of the term. Here, as the understanding cannot provide sufficient reason for the act of faith, the entire will is shot through with an inner, supernatural light named grace. We may perhaps be scandalized to see this autonomous, infinite freedom suddenly *affected* by divine grace and *disposed* to affirm what it does not see clearly. But is there ultimately any great difference between natural light and this supernatural light that is grace? In the latter case, it is absolutely certain that it is God who does the affirming, employing the intermediary of our will. But is this not also true in the former case? If ideas have being, they do so insofar as they come from God. Clarity and distinctness are merely the signs of the inner cohesion and absolute density of being of the idea. And if I am irresistibly inclined to affirm the idea, I am so precisely insofar as it weighs on me with all its being and absolute positivity. It is this pure, dense, flawless, full being that asserts itself within me by its own influence. Thus, since God is the source of all being and all positivity, a true judgement, which is positivity and fullness of existence, necessarily has its source not in me, who am nothing, but in Him. And we shouldn't see this theory merely as an effort to reconcile a rationalist metaphysics with Christian theology: it expresses, in the vocabulary of the day, the awareness the scientist has always had of being pure nothingness, a mere beholder of the stubborn, eternal consistency and infinite gravity of the truth he contemplates. Admittedly, three years later in 1644 Descartes came back to the question, this time conceding the freedom of indifference:

> We are so conscious of the freedom and indifference which are in us, that there is nothing which we understand more clearly; so that the omnipotence of God should not keep us from believing it.[11]

But this is a mere precaution: the enormous success of the *Augustinus* had made him anxious and he didn't want to risk being condemned at the Sorbonne.[12] We should, rather, point out that this new conception of freedom without free will now extended to all areas of his thinking. Does he not, indeed, say to Mersenne:

> You reject what I say, namely that it is enough to judge well to act well; and yet it seems to me that the ordinary doctrine of the Schoolmen is that *Voluntas non fertur in malum, nisi quatenus*

11 René Descartes, *Principles of Philosophy* (Dordrecht: Kluwer Academic Publishers, 1984), p. 19 (translation modified; Sartre is quoting from the French translation with additions and corrections by Descartes himself, whereas the Kluwer edition is based on the original Latin text [Trans.]).

12 The reference is the posthumously published *magnum opus* of the Bishop of Ypres, Cornelius Otto Jansen, entitled *Augustinus, seu doctrina S. Augustini de humanae naturae sanitate, aegritudine, medicina, adversus Pelagianos et Massilienses* (Leuven/Louvain, 1640). [Trans.]

*ei sub aliqua ratione boni repraesentatur ab intel-lectu.*[13] Hence the saying, *omnis peccans est igno-rans*; with the result that, so long as the understanding never represented something to the will as good which was not, the will could not fail in its choosing.[14]

The argument is now complete: the clear vision of the Good entails the act in the same way as the distinct vision of the True entails assent. For the Good and the True are one and the same thing: namely, Being. And if Descartes can say that we are never so free as when we do Good, he is here substituting a definition of freedom by the *value* of acts—the freest act being the best, the most in keeping with the universal order—for a defini-tion in terms of autonomy. And this accords with the logic of his doctrine: if we don't invent *our own* Good, if the Good has an *a priori*, independent existence, how could we see it and not do it?

Yet in the search for the True, as in the pursuit of Good, we find a genuine human autonomy. But only inso-far as the human being is nothing. It is by his nothing-ness, and inasmuch as he has dealings with Nothingness, Evil and Error that man escapes God, for God, who is infinite fullness of being, cannot either conceive or

---

13 The will does not incline towards evil, except insofar as that evil is represented by the understanding as being in some way good. [Trans.]

14 René Descartes, 'A Mersenne' (27 april 1637?), in *Oeuvres et lettres*, p. 963.

govern nothingness. He has put the positive in me: he is the author responsible for everything in me that *is*. But by my finitude and limitedness, by my shadow side, I turn away from Him. If I retain a freedom of indifference, I do so in relation to what I do not know or what I know poorly, in relation to truncated, mutilated or confused ideas. To all these nothings, I can, as a nothing myself, say *no*: I *am able not to* decide to act or affirm. Since the order of truths exists outside me, what will define me as autonomy isn't creative invention, but refusal. It is by refusing until we can refuse no longer that we are free. Thus methodical doubt becomes the very model of the free act: '*Nihilominus . . . hanc in nobis libertatem esse experimur, ut semper ab iis credendis, quae non plane certa sunt et explorata possimus abstinere.*'[15] And elsewhere: '*Mens quae propria libertate utens supponit ea omnia non existere, de quarum existentia vel minimum potest dubitare.*'[16]

The reader will recognize something like a foreshadowing of Hegelian negativity in this power to escape, to disengage oneself and to withdraw. All propositions

---

15 'We nonetheless experience in ourselves a freedom such that we can always abstain from believing those things which are not absolutely certain and established.' From René Descartes, *Principles of Philosophy*, Part 1, Section 6 (Dordrecht: Kluwer, 1991), p. 4.

16 'The mind uses its own freedom and supposes the non-existence of all the things about whose existence it can have even the slightest doubt.' From René Descartes, 'Synopsis of the following six meditations', in *Meditations on First Philosophy*, p. 9. See also René Descartes, 'Abrégé des Six Méditations suivantes', in *Oeuvres et lettres*, p. 262. [Trans.]

asserting something outside of our thought are tinged with doubt; in other words, I can bracket out all existents and I am exercising my freedom to the full when I, myself an empty nothingness, *void* everything that exists. Doubt is a breaking of contact with being; through it man has the permanent possibility of extricating himself from the existing universe and suddenly contemplating it from on high as a pure succession of phantasms. It is, in this sense, the most magnificent affirmation of the reign of the human: the hypothesis of the Evil Genius shows clearly that man can escape all deceptions and traps; there is an order of truth because man is free; and even if that order didn't exist, it would be sufficient that man was free for there never to be a reign of error. This is because man, being this pure negation, this pure suspension of judgement, may, so long as he remains motionless, like someone holding his breath, withdraw at any moment from a false, fake nature; he can even withdraw from all that is nature within him: from his memory, imagination and body. He can withdraw from time itself and take refuge in the eternity of the moment: nothing reveals better than this that man isn't a 'natural' being. But at the point when he achieves this unparalleled independence, against the omnipotence of the Evil Genius, and even against God, he catches himself being pure nothingness: over against the *being* that is entirely bracketed out, all that remains is a mere *no* that has neither body nor memory, knowledge nor *personhood*. And it is this translucent rejection of everything that is itself attained in the *cogito*, as is shown by the following passage: '*Dubito ergo sum, vel, quod idem est: Cogito ergo sum.*'[17] Even though this doctrine takes its inspiration from the Stoic *epoche*, no one before Descartes had put the emphasis on the link between free will and negativity; no one had shown that freedom in no sense comes from man insofar as he is a fullness of existence among other fullnesses in a flawless world, but insofar as he *is not*, insofar as he is finite and limited. But this freedom cannot in any way be creative, since it is *nothing*. It doesn't possess the power to produce an idea, since an idea is a reality; in other words, an idea possesses a certain *being* that I cannot impart to it. Moreover, Descartes will himself limit its scope, since in his view, when being finally appears—absolute, prefect, infinitely infinite being—we cannot refuse it our adherence. We see at this point that he hasn't taken his theory of negativity to its limit, 'since truth consists in *being* and falsehood in *non-being* only'.[18] The power of refusal that is in man consists solely in rejecting the false—in short, in saying no to non-being. If we can withhold our assent from the works of the Evil Genius, this is not in any sense insofar as they *are* (i.e. insofar as, true or false, they have at least, inasmuch

17 'I doubt, therefore I am or, which is the same thing, I think, therefore I am.' See René Descartes, 'La Recherche de la vérité par la lumière naturelle', in *Oeuvres et lettres*, p. 898. [Trans.]

18 Letter to Clerselier, 23 April 1649.

as they *are* our representations, a minimum of being) but insofar as they *are not*—that is to say, insofar as they refer mendaciously to objects that don't exist. If we can withdraw from the world, we can do so not inasmuch as it exists in its full, lofty majesty as an absolute affirmation, but inasmuch as it appears to us confusedly by way of our senses and we conceive it imperfectly through a number of ideas whose foundations are beyond our grasp. Thus Descartes is perpetually wavering between the identification of freedom with the negativity or negation of being—which can be described as the freedom of indifference—and the conception of free will as mere negation of the negation. In a word, he failed to conceive negativity as productive.

A strange freedom. It breaks down, ultimately, into two phases: in the first, it is negative and this represents an autonomy, but it boils down merely to refusing to assent to error or to confused thought; in the second phase, it changes meaning and is a positive adherence, but the will loses its autonomy at that point and the great clarity that is in the understanding penetrates and determines the will. Is this really Descartes's intention and does the theory he constructed really correspond to the initial sense this proud, independent man had of his free will? It does not seem so. First, whether he is going back over the history of his thinking, as in the *Discourse on the Method* or encountering himself as an unshakable fact on the path of his doubt, this individualist, whose very person plays such a role in his philosophy, conceived a disembodying, de-individualizing freedom. For, if we are to believe him, the thinking subject is initially *nothing* but pure negation; that nothingness, that little quivering of air that alone escapes the enterprise of doubting and is *nothing other* than doubt itself; and when it moves out of that nothingness, it does so to become pure assumption of being. There isn't much difference between the Cartesian scientist, who is ultimately the mere *vision* of eternal truths, and the Platonic philosopher, dead to his body and dead to his life, who is nothing but the contemplation of Forms and in the end equates himself with science itself. But *the man* in Descartes had other ambitions: he viewed his life as an enterprise; he wanted science to be *done* and to be done by him, but his freedom didn't allow him to 'do' it. His wish was that people would cultivate their passions, provided they made good use of them: he glimpsed, so to speak, the paradoxical truth that there are *free* passions. Above all he prized true generosity, which he defined in the following terms:

> I believe that true Generosity, which makes a man esteem himself as highly as he can legitimately esteem himself, consists only in this: partly in his understanding that there is nothing which truly belongs to him but this free control of his volitions, and no reason why he ought to be praised or blamed except that he uses it well or badly; and partly in his feeling within himself

a firm and constant resolution to use it well, that is, never to lack the volition to undertake and execute all the things he judges to be best— which is to follow virtue perfectly.[19]

Yet this freedom he invented, which can hold back desires only until the clear sight of the Good determines the resolutions of the will, cannot bear out this proud sense of being the true author of his acts and the continual initiator of free undertakings, any more than it can give him the means of inventing operational schemes in accordance with the general rules of the Method. This is because Descartes, dogmatic scientist and good Christian that he is, allows himself to be crushed by the pre-established order of eternal verities and the eternal system of values created by God. If he doesn't invent his own Good, if he doesn't construct Science, man is free in name alone. And Cartesian freedom here is like Christian freedom, which is a false freedom: Cartesian man and Christian man are both free for Evil, not for Good; they are free for Error, not for Truth. By way of the natural and supernatural light he dispenses to them, God leads them by the hand towards Knowledge and Virtue, which He has chosen for them; they simply have to let themselves be led; the entire merit in their ascension is His. But, inasmuch as they are nothingness, they escape His grasp; they are free to let go his hand along

19 Descartes, *The Passions of the Soul*, p. 104.

the way and plunge into the world of sin and non-being. On the other hand, of course, they can always choose to keep themselves from intellectual and moral Evil: keep and preserve themselves, suspend their judgement, suppress their desires and halt their actions in time. All that is asked of them, ultimately, isn't to thwart God's intentions. But, in the end, Error and Evil are forms of non-being: man doesn't even have the freedom to produce anything on that terrain. If he persists in his vice and his prejudices, what he creates will be a *nothing*; the universal order will not even be troubled by their obstinacy. 'The worst,' says Claudel, 'is not always certain.' In a doctrine that confuses being and perception, the only field of human initiative is the 'bastard' terrain Plato speaks of that is 'glimpsed only in dreams', the frontier between being and non-being.

However, since Descartes notifies us that God's freedom is no more entire than that of man and that the one is in the image of the other, we have a new means of investigation available to us for determining more exactly the exigencies within himself that philosophical postulates didn't enable him to satisfy. If he conceived divine freedom as very similar to his own, then it is of his own freedom, as he would have conceived it without the fetters of Catholicism and dogmatism, that he speaks when he describes God's freedom. There is an obvious phenomenon of sublimation and transposition in this. Now, Descartes's God is the freest of the Gods forged by human thought; he is the only creative God. In fact, he is subject neither to principles—even the principle of identity—nor to a sovereign Good that he would merely be bringing about. He didn't merely create existents according to rules that might be said to have imposed themselves on his will, but he created both beings and their essences, the world and the world's laws, individuals and first principles.

> Mathematical truths, which you call 'eternal', were established by God, and depend on him entirely, like all other created beings. In truth, it would be speaking of God like a Jupiter or Saturn, making him subject to Styx and the Fates, to say that these truths are independent of him. . . . [I]t is God who set up these laws in nature, as a king sets up laws in his kingdom.[20]

As for the eternal truths, I say once more that they are true or possible only because God knows them as true or possible; they are not, contrariwise, known to God as true as though they were true independently of him. And if men properly understood the sense of their words, they could never say without blasphemy that the truth about something is antecedent to God's knowledge of it; for in God knowing and willing are but one thing; so that from the very fact of his willing something, He

---

20 René Descartes, 'Descartes to Mersenne, 15 April 1630', in *Philosophical Writings*, p. 259.

knows it, and for this reason alone is such a thing true. We must not say, then, that if God did not exist, nevertheless these truths would be true.[21]

> [Y]ou ask what made it necessary for God to create these truths. What I say is that God was just as much free to make it untrue that all straight lines drawn from centre to circumference are equal, as he was not to create the world. And certainly these truths are not necessarily conjoined with God's essence any more than other creatures are.[22]

> Moreover that God wished some truths to be necessary does not mean that he necessarily wished them; for it is one thing to wish them to be necessary and quite another to wish it necessarily or to be the necessity of wishing it.[23]

The meaning of the Cartesian doctrine reveals itself here. Descartes understood perfectly that the concept of freedom included the demand for absolute autonomy, that a free act was an absolutely new product, the germ of which couldn't be contained in an antecedent state of

21 René Descartes, 'Descartes to Mersenne, 6 May 1630', in *Philosophical Writings*, pp. 260–1.

22 René Descartes, 'Descartes to Mersenne, 27 May 1630, in *Philosophical Writings*, p. 262. The date of this letter is misprinted in the English source. [Trans.]

23 René Descartes, 'Au Père Mesland' (2 May 1644?), in *Oeuvres et lettres*, p. 1167.

the world, and that consequently freedom and creation were one and the same. God's freedom, though similar to man's, loses the negative aspect it had within its human shell; it is pure productivity; it is the extra-temporal, eternal act by which God brings a world, a 'Good', and eternal Truths into being. Henceforth, the root of all Reason is to be found in the depths of the free act; it is freedom that is the foundation of the true; the rigorous necessity that appears in the order of truths is itself subtended by the absolute contingency of a creative free will, and this dogmatic rationalist might, like Goethe, say not 'In the beginning was the Word', but 'In the beginning was the Deed.' As for the difficulty of maintaining freedom in the face of truth, he glimpsed a solution in a conception of creation that was simultaneously an intellection, as though the thing created by free decree stood, so to speak, before the freedom that keeps it in being and, in the same process, yielded itself up for comprehension. In God, will and intuition are one; the divine consciousness is both constitutive and contemplative. And, similarly, God invented Good. His perfection does not incline him to decide what is best; rather, what he has decided is, by the very effect of his deciding it, absolutely good. An absolute freedom that invents Reason and Good and has no other limits than itself and being true to itself—this is, in the end, the divine prerogative so far as Descartes is concerned. On the other hand, there is no more in this freedom than in human freedom, and he is aware, in describing the free will of his God, of merely having developed the implicit content of the idea of freedom. This is why, all things considered, human freedom isn't limited by an order of freedoms and values that might be said to offer themselves up for our assent as eternal *things*, as necessary structures of being. It is the divine will that has laid down these values and truths; it is that will that sustains them: our freedom is bounded by divine freedom only. The world is merely the creation of a freedom that preserves it indefinitely; truth is nothing unless it is willed by this infinite divine power, and unless it is taken up and confirmed by human freedom. The free man stands alone over against an absolutely free God; freedom is the ground of being, its secret dimension; in this rigorous system, it is, in the end, the profound meaning and true face of necessity.

So Descartes, in his description of divine freedom, eventually returns to, and clarifies, his initial intuition of his own freedom, which, as he said, 'is known without proof and merely by our experience of it'.[24] It is of little consequence to us that he was forced by his times—and also by his starting point—to reduce human free will to a merely negative power to deny itself, until finally it yields and abandons itself to divine solicitude; it is of

---

24 These lines provide the heading of Section 39 of Part 1 of Descartes's *Principles of Philosophy*, published originally in Latin at Amsterdam in 1644 and translated into French in 1647. See Descartes, *Oeuvres et Lettres*, p. 588. [Trans.]

little consequence to us that he hypostasized in God this original, *constituent* freedom, the infinite existence of which he grasped by way of the *cogito* itself: the fact remains that a formidable power of divine and human affirmation runs through his universe and sustains it. It would take two crisis-ridden centuries—a crisis of Faith and a crisis of Science—for humanity to take back this creative freedom that Descartes vested in God, and for us at last to surmise the truth, which is the essential basis of humanism, that man is the being whose emergence causes a world to exist. But we shall not criticize Descartes for having vested in God what properly belongs to us; we shall, rather, admire him for having, in an authoritarian age, laid the groundwork for democracy, for having fully followed through the exigencies of the idea of *autonomy* and for having understood, long before the Heidegger of *Vom Wesen des Grundes*, that the sole ground of being was freedom.[25]

---

25 Simone Pétrement takes me to task in *Critique* for having overlooked 'freedom against oneself' in this article. The fact is that she isn't, herself, familiar with the dialectic of freedom. Freedom against *oneself* does, of course, exist. And the self is *nature* from the standpoint of the freedom that wishes to change it. But for it to be 'self', it must first be freedom. Nature is, otherwise, mere exteriority and hence radical negation of the person. Even *helpless confusion* [*le désarroi*]—in other words, the inner imitation of exteriority—and even *alienation* presuppose freedom.

※

# A FUNDAMENTAL IDEA
# OF HUSSERL'S PHENOMENOLOGY:
## INTENTIONALITY

'He devoured her with his eyes.' This phrase and many other indications point up to some extent the illusion, common to both realism and idealism, that to know is to eat. After a hundred years of academicism, French philosophy is still at this point. We have all read Brunschvicg, Lalande and Meyerson;[1] we all once believed that the Spider-Mind attracted things into its web, covered them with a white spittle and slowly ingested them, reducing them to its own substance. What is a table, a rock or a house? A certain assemblage of 'contents of consciousness', an ordering of those contents. Oh alimentary

---

1 Léon Brunschvicg (1869–1944), André Lalande (1867–1963) and Émile Meyerson (1859–1933): prominent academic philosophers whose work had largely passed out of vogue by Sartre's day. [Trans.]

philosophy! Yet nothing seemed more obvious: isn't the table the current content of my perception? Isn't perception the present state of my consciousness? Nutrition, assimilation. The assimilation, as Lalande said, of things to ideas, of ideas among themselves and of minds between themselves. The powerful bones of the world were picked apart by these painstaking diastases: assimilation, unification and identification. In vain did the simplest and coarsest of us search for something solid, something that was not, ultimately, mere mind. But they encountered everywhere an insubstantial, though very distinguished, mist: themselves.

Against the digestive philosophy of empiriocriticism and neo-Kantianism and all forms of 'psychologism', Husserl never tires of asserting that one cannot dissolve things in consciousness. Admittedly, you see this tree here. But you see it at the place where it is: beside the road, amid the dust, standing alone and distorted in the heat, twenty leagues from the Mediterranean coast. It cannot enter your consciousness, because it is not of the same nature as consciousness. You think you recognize Bergson's position in the first chapter of *Matter and Memory* here. But Husserl isn't in any way a realist: he doesn't make this tree, standing on its bit of cracked earth, an absolute that would subsequently enter into communication with us. Consciousness and the world are given at a single stroke: the world, external by its essence to consciousness is, by its essence, relative to consciousness. This is because Husserl sees consciousness as an irreducible fact, which no physical image can render. Except, perhaps, the rapid, obscure image of bursting. To know is to 'burst out towards', to wrest oneself from moist, gastric intimacy and fly out over there, beyond oneself, to what is not oneself. To fly over there, to the tree, and yet outside the tree, because it eludes and repels me and I can no more lose myself in it than it can dissolve itself into me: outside it, outside myself. Don't you recognize your own exigencies and sense of things in this description? You knew very well that the tree wasn't you, that you couldn't take it inside your dark stomach, and that knowledge couldn't, without dishonesty, be compared to possession. And, in this same process, consciousness is purified and becomes clear as a great gust of wind. There is nothing in it any more, except an impulse to flee itself, a sliding outside of itself. If, impossibly, you were to 'enter' a consciousness, you would be picked up by a whirlwind and thrown back outside to where the tree is and all the dust, for consciousness has no 'inside'. It is merely the exterior of itself and it is this absolute flight, this refusal to be substance, that constitute it as a consciousness. Imagine now a linked series of bursts that wrest us from ourselves, that do not even leave an 'ourself' the time to form behind them, but rather hurl us out beyond them into the dry dust of the world, on to the rough earth, among things. Imagine we are thrown out in this way, abandoned by our very natures in an indifferent, hostile, resistant world. If you do so, you will have grasped the profound meaning of the discovery Husserl expresses in this famous phrase: 'All consciousness is consciousness *of* something.' This is all it takes to put an end to the cosy philosophy of immanence, in which everything works by compromise, by protoplasmic exchanges, by a tepid cellular chemistry. The philosophy of transcendence throws us out on to the high road, amid threats and under a blinding light. Being, says Heidegger, is being-in-the-world. This 'being-in' is to be understood in the sense of movement. To be is to burst forth into the world. It is to start out from a nothingness-of-world-and-consciousness and suddenly to burst-out-as-consciousness-in-the-world. If consciousness attempts to regain control of itself, to coincide, at long last, with itself, in a nice warm room with the shutters closed, it annihilates itself. Husserl calls this need on the part of consciousness to exist as consciousness of something other than itself 'intentionality'.

If I have spoken, first, of knowledge, I have done so to gain a better hearing: the French philosophy that shaped us is almost totally confined now to epistemology. But, for Husserl and the phenomenologists, the consciousness we have of things is not in any way limited to mere knowledge of them. Knowledge or 'pure' representation is only one of the possible forms of my consciousness *of* this tree. I may also love it, fear it, hate it, and this surpassing of consciousness by itself that we call intentionality turns up again in fear, hatred and love. To hate another person is one more way of bursting out towards him; it is to find oneself suddenly faced with a stranger whose objective 'hateful' quality one experiences or, rather, first suffers. Suddenly, then, these famous 'subjective' reactions of love and loathing, fear and liking, which were floating around in the foul-smelling brine of the Mind, tear themselves away from it; they are merely ways of discovering the world. It is things that suddenly disclose themselves to us as hateful, pleasant, horrible or lovable. Fearsomeness is a *property* of this Japanese mask, an inexhaustible, irreducible property that constitutes its very nature—not the sum of our subjective reactions to a piece of carved wood. Husserl has put horror and charm back into things. He has given us back the world of artists and prophets: terrifying, hostile and dangerous, with havens of grace and love. He has cleared the way for a new Treatise of Passions that would take its inspiration from this very simple truth that is so poorly understood by our finest minds: if we love a woman, it is because she is lovable. We can leave Proust behind now. And, with him,  the 'inner life': in vain would we seek, like Amiel,[2] or like a child kissing her own shoulder, the caresses and fondlings of a private intimacy, since, at long last, everything is outside. Everything, including ourselves. It is outside, in the world,

---

2 Henri-Frédéric Amiel (1821–81): Swiss philosopher and diarist. [Trans.]

among others. It is not in some lonely refuge that we shall discover ourselves, but on the road, in the town, in the crowd, as a thing among things and a human being among human beings.

*January 1939*

＊

## THERE AND BACK[1]

Parain is a man on the move. He hasn't arrived yet, nor does he even know precisely where he wants to get to, but we can get a general sense of his direction of travel. I would describe it as a return. He himself entitled one of his works *Retour à la France* and, in that book, he wrote:

> I have learned, after a long period of uncon-
> straint, that the mediating powers have the role
> of forbidding man to step outside his domain.
> At his extreme limits, they set up barriers,
> beyond which destruction threatens him.

---

1 On Brice Parain, *Recherches sur la nature et les fonctions du langage* (Paris: Gallimard, 1942). Parain (1897–1971), a great friend of Albert Camus, was an essayist whose work was so characterized by a deep concern for the particularities of language that the critic Charles Blanchard dubbed him 'the Sherlock Holmes of language'. Parain was a committed Communist and lived for a time in the USSR after World War I; he was no longer so when he wrote *Retour à la France*. [Trans.]

These few words might be enough to date his undertaking: he journeyed to the extremes, tried to step outside of himself, and now he is coming back. Isn't this the entire literary history of the post-war period? People had great, inhuman ambitions. The aim was to grasp nature—both within man and outside him—as it was when human beings were absent from it; one tiptoed into the garden to catch it unawares and see it at last as it was when there was no one there to see it. And then, somewhere around the 1930s, encouraged and urged on by publishers, journalists and picture dealers—and channelled through them—came the beginnings of a return to the human. A return to order. The aim now was to define a modest, practical wisdom in which contemplation would be subordinated to limited, effective action and the ambitious values of truth would yield to those of honesty; it was a wisdom that wasn't a pragmatism, nor an opportunism, but a new mix of values, illuminating action with knowledge and subordinating knowledge to action, subjecting the individual to the social order and yet refusing to sacrifice him to it; in short, an economical wisdom whose main concern was to strike a balance.

I fear that the youngest among us have gone far beyond it today: events seem to require both less and more. But it was, after all, an adventure of the mind, as valid as all the others, such as Surrealism or Gidean individualism, and one to be judged, in times to come, by its consequences. In any event, it was through this adventure—and in it—that Parain chose who he was to be. There is, however, something we must be clear about: there have been some fake 'returns'. Some, like Schlumberger,[2] who believed they had never left, merely wanted to force others to return. 'We must turn around and go back,' they said, but it was evident that the 'we' was just a polite formula. A sad, severe younger generation, conscious of the shortness of their lives, hastily took their places in the marching troop—a group who, as the popular quip has it, 'have lost all their illusions, without ever having had any in the first place'. We even saw a curious species of sad *arriviste*, a thin-blooded Julien Sorel,[3] like Petitjean, who exploited this deflation to make his bid for success.[4] For his part, Parain made a genuine return. He knew and experienced the temptation of the inhuman and now he is returning slowly and clumsily to human beings, with memories the young do not possess. Think of the 'return' of Aragon and his

2 Jean Schlumberger (1877–1968): a French author and publisher, and one of the founders, with Gide among others, of the *Nouvelle Revue Française*. [Trans.]

3 Julien Sorel is the central character in Stendhal's 1830 novel, *Le Rouge et le Noir* (variously translated as *The Red and the Black*, *The Scarlet and the Black*, etc.). [Trans.]

4 Armand-Marcel Petitjean (1913–2003): son of the founder of the Lancôme perfume company, he had some success as an avant-garde writer and essayist in the 1930s. Though an anti-fascist in the pre-war period, Petitjean went over to Marshal Pétain's 'National Revolution' during the Occupation. [Trans.]

new arthritic Surrealist style,[5] shot through with sudden bolts of lightning that recall the extravagances of yesteryear; think of the 'return' of La Fresnaye,[6] coming back from Cubism and eliciting a timid, hesitant meaning from the stony faces he paints. Parain is their brother. But his bouts of excess and repentance, his fits of anger and despair were always worked out between himself and language. We should, then, see the *Recherches sur la nature et les fonctions du langage* as a stage in a return to order or, more accurately, in a *re-descent*. He writes:

> You climb up to the plateau to see as far as is possible; you climb up to the plateau, where the wind blows . . . where life is solitary . . . You go back down to the valley, back to sea level, to gardens and houses, to where the farrier and wheelwright are, below the cemetery and the church; you go back down for evening, as the darkness begins to fall . . . Everything climbs up out of the valley and returns to the valley.[7]

It is this itinerary we are going to attempt to retrace, step by step. First the ascent, then the re-descent. Parain is a

---

5 Louis Aragon (1897–1982): one of the greatest French poets and novelists of the twentieth century. [Trans.]

6 Roger de la Fresnaye (1885–1925): a French painter associated successively with the Section d'Or and Puteaux groups of artists. He moved away from the Cubist style decisively after World War I, though by then his health was failing badly. [Trans.]

7 Brice Parain, *Retour à la France* (Paris: Grasset, 1936). Sartre gives no page number. [Trans.]

lyrical writer: by a very peculiar stroke of good fortune, despite having more concern for others than for himself, this honest, good man, with his precise, impartial intelligence, nonetheless speaks about himself. And this is the case whatever he may say, and even if he does not realize it. But, you will say, that is true of everyone. And so it is. But at least his testimony is perfectly decipherable: we shall draw on it to reconstitute the history of this great re-descent, sadder than a bout of despair, which, after what Daniel-Rops termed the 'turning years' of the late twenties and early thirties,[8] characterized the second half of the post-war period.

## I. INTUITION

In Parain's journey, the departure is marked by an intuition, while an experience initiates the return. When, at the age of twenty-five, one writes of 'the signs establishing imperfect communication between men, governing social relations in the manner of a shaky lever',[9] and, twelve years later, that

> There is just one problem . . . the problem posed by the non-necessity of language. Through it human energy seems not to transmit itself fully

---

8 Henri Daniel-Rops (1901–65): French novelist, social theorist and historian.[Trans.]

9 Brice Parain, *Essai sur la misère humaine* (Paris: Grasset, 1934). Sartre again gives no page number. [Trans.]

as it goes through its transformations . . . There's
too much play in the gears,[10]

then one offers a fine example of consistency of thinking
and persistence in one's metaphors. The fact is these
comparisons express a fundamental intuition which
Parain, in *Essai sur la Misère humaine*, calls: 'the dizzying
sense of language's inexactness'. This tells us what we
need to know: Parain doesn't begin his research with the
inhuman impartiality of the linguist. He is suffering
from word-sickness and wants to be cured. He feels out
of phase with language.

That is enough to tell us that this is not the place to
be looking for an an objective study of linguistic sounds.
The linguist usually acts like a man who is confident
in his ideas, concerned only to know whether language,
an ancient traditional institution, renders them with
precision. So, for example, the 'parallelism' between logic
and grammar will be studied, as though logic were given,
on the one hand, in the heaven of ideas, and grammar
were given on earth. A French equivalent for the German
word *Stimmung* will be sought, for example, which
assumes that the corresponding notion exists for a French
speaker as it does for a German, and all that arises is
the question of its expression. But language regarded in
this way is anonymous: the words are thrown on the
table like dead fish, already killed and cooked. In short,
the linguist studies language when no one is speaking

10 Unpublished manuscript of November 1922.

it. Dead words, dead concepts. He studies the word 'Freedom' as you might fish it out of texts, not the living, intoxicating, irritating, lethal word as it resonates today in an angry or an eager mouth. Parain, by contrast, is concerned with language 'as it is spoken'. In other words, he sees it as a link in the chain of concrete action. What he grapples with is the language of this particular soldier or worker or revolutionary. In this sense, how can words be distinguished from ideas? The orator speaks and says 'Justice' or 'Democracy' and the whole auditorium applauds. Which part of this is the 'thought' and which the 'verbal material'? What strikes the listener is the whole thing together: what Claudel so felicitously calls 'the intelligible mouthful'. And it is this intelligible mouthful that Parain will examine. 'Words are ideas,' he writes in *Recherches*, for he has already adopted a practical, political perspective, as has Heidegger, who refuses to distinguish between body and soul, a problem of contemplative philosophy, and who would happily write that, from the point of view of action, which is the only real standpoint, the soul is the body and the body is the soul. As a peasant, an 'assiduous warrior' of World War I and a citizen, Parain deliberately rejects the joys of contemplation. His first—unpublished—essay was concerned with the pursuit of an 'art of living'. 'War,' he wrote, 'has made us see the value of life, and has shown us not to waste a single moment of it.' Since then, morality and politics, indissolubly linked, are his great concern. 'A theory of knowledge,' he writes in 1934, 'can only ever be a theory of the reform of the understanding and, in the end, a treatise on morality.' And by this he meant to underline that he granted primacy to the *practical* sphere over all others. Man is a being who acts. Science, metaphysics and language have their scope and meaning within the narrow limits of that action. One might be tempted to compare Parain with Auguste Comte: they share a lapidary, forceful sense of seriousness, a determination not to distinguish morality from politics, and a deep sense of human solidarity. But Comte is an engineer. Behind his theory of action, we sense the machine-tool or the locomotive. Parain is of peasant stock; he was, like all the men of the 1920s, fired with a great anger against machinism. Behind his morality and his critique of language, we glimpse the pick and the shovel, the workbench. In any event, the two thinkers have the same concern to think their age through and to do so with ideas that are 'of the times'; they distrust the universal and the eternal. It is the language of 1940 that Parain studies, not universal language. It is language with its sick words, in which 'Peace' means aggression, 'Freedom' oppression and 'Socialism' a regime of social inequality. And if he examines those words, he does so not as a biologist but as a doctor. By this I mean that it is not his aim to isolate organs and examine them in a laboratory; it is the whole organism that he studies and intends to cure.

'It wasn't I,' writes Parain, 'who invented the distrust of language . . . We have been fed it by the whole of our civilization.'[11] It is his intention, thereby, to date his investigations in the same way as Hegel dated Hegelianism. But this dating is too crude an approximation. For you are not the author of the *Recherches*—and neither am I. You may perhaps be too old and I am a little too young. Look at the thinkers who came out of this last war: they praise Parain; they approve of what he is doing. But they no longer entirely understand him, and they inflect his findings towards their own ends—Blanchot, for example, using them for purposes of political protest. If we want to understand his message fully, we must bear in mind that it comes from a man of the inter-war years. It is, then, arriving slightly belatedly; it wasn't transmitted at the appointed time—just like the work of Proust, written before the 1914 war and read after it—and it is this delay, this slight dissonance that no doubt makes it so fruitful. Parain is a man of forty-six. He is a peasant who was sent to the front in the last years of the first war: it is this that will explain his original intuition to us.

The peasant works alone amid the forces of nature, which act without any need of being named. He says nothing. Parain has written of his 'stupour' when he gets back to the village after ploughing his field and hears human voices. He has written, too, of the

> social destruction of the individual which . . .
> tends to continue today in the transformation
> of the peasant into an agricultural worker . . .

---

11 Parain, *Essai sur la misère humaine*, pp. 157–8.

> For a peasant, the earth is the intermediary that binds his thought solidly to his action and enables him to judge and act . . . For a worker or for any member of industrial civilization, this bond or intercessor is the plan, the scientific hypothesis of construction that provides him with the idea of his place in the whole and assigns him his collective usefulness, his social and inner value. It is language that is the vehicle of intelligence. In moving . . . from the field that is to be tilled to the part that is to be manufactured, we move from a thinking that is more concrete and closer to its object to a thought that is more abstract and further iremoved from its object.[12]

Like so many others, Parain came into the city. But what he encountered there first wasn't the technical language of the factories and building sites, but rhetoric. At the École Normale Supérieure, I knew many of these peasants' sons, who had been wrested from the soil by their exceptional intelligence. For long periods, they were as silent as the soil, but would suddenly break that silence to expatiate on the most abstract subjects. Like the Socrates of *The Clouds*, they would argue both sides of the case with equal virtuosity and a pedantry that was its own source of amusement. And then they would sink back into silence. Visibly, this intellectual

---

12 Parain, *Essai sur la misère humaine*, p. 99.

gymnastics remained something alien; it was merely a game to them, a murmur of noise on the surface of their silence. Parain was one such student. In November 1922 (he had just sat the *agrégation* in philosophy), he himself wrote: 'I have at last completed my studies in a University where the art of persuasion has replaced the art of living and thinking.' He was taught at that time the brilliant, weightless language of polemic. A young worker has to decide for or against Marx. Parain didn't have to decide between Voltaire and Rousseau, but he knew how properly to compare them, reconcile them or condemn them both equally. He has remained a formidable dialectician. He has the art of responding quickly and sharply, of going off at a tangent, breaking off a line of thought, or halting a discussion with a single word when he is in difficulty. But he *hears himself* speak, with a kind of scandalized amusement. He hears himself speak from the depths of his silence. And this affords an initial distance with regard to language. He will always see words through a layer of dumbness, the way fish probably see bathers on the surface of the water. 'When we understand each other well,' he says, 'we remain silent.' At home, he remains silent. What is there to say? One person is repairing a wobbly table, another is sewing; the house is there around them. This alternative between quickfire speech and silence is a characteristic feature of his person. In 1922 he calls this mutism *instinct* and contrasts it with speech, which is 'eloquence' or 'polemic'. 'When we understand each other well, we remain silent.' The lamp is on the table; everyone is working and senses the mute presence of the others: there is an order of silence. Later, for Parain, there will be an order of instinct. As for these little verbal cracklings on his surface, they are not his. They have been given—or, rather, lent—to him. They come from the town. In the fields and the house, they are redundant.

This peasant fought in the war, which is another factor setting him apart. The unified language he had just learned in the town, that language of academics and industrialists, seemed to him, in a way, like an impersonal Reason in which every individual could participate. The war taught Parain there were several Reasons—the reason of the Germans, that of the Russians and ours—and that each corresponds to an objective system of signs and that they are all engaged in a trial of strength. He learned this lesson amid a new silence, full of explosions and violent wrenches, amid a mute solidarity. Words still run along the surface of this silence. Articles by Barrès,[13] communiqués, patriotic speeches really become 'words' for these men standing silent in their trenches. They are 'words, words!' They have lost their affective roots and no longer culminate in action. But this ineffectuality unmasks them. When a word is a link in a chain—'pass me the . . . there . . .'—it fades from view; you obey it without

---

13 Maurice Barrès (1862–1923): a novelist, journalist and political activist; close to the Symbolist movement in his youth, he came to be associated with extreme nationalism and a current of pre-fascist romanticism in early-twentieth-century French literature. [Trans.]

hearing it or seeing it. But when it is no longer the vehicle of anything, it displays and reveals itself *as word*, in the same way as, for Bergson, it is indetermination in reaction that carves out an image of the world. It is this language, still fully armed, fully alive, coming warm out of human mouths, this language cut off from any practical application and all the more haunting for that, which will, from this point on, be the subject of Parain's studies. I was saying just now that he didn't wish to carry out the linguist's dessicating experiments on words, that he refused to form them arbitrarily into an isolated system. But events effected for him what in methodology is called a 'passive experiment'. The word isolated itself of itself, spontaneously, while retaining nonetheless a human flavour. For the peasant that was Parain, language was, until not so long ago, the town. Now, for the soldier, it is 'the home front'.

And then back he comes. As though his whole life were to have this there-and-back rhythm to it. The return of the young intellectual to the fields for his holidays; the return of the demobilized soldier to Paris for Peace. And it was a return to put language to the test once more. All the words were there around him as willing servants; he had only to take them. And yet as soon as he wanted to use them, they betrayed him. When it comes to describing to women or old men what the war was like, he has only to reach out his hand: the words 'horror', 'terror', 'boredom', etc., will be there for the taking. But, like the message in *Aminadab* that changes meaning as it is passed along, the words are not understood in the sense in which they were meant. What does 'terror' mean to a woman? And what is boredom? How is one to insert into language an experience that was had without it? He will at least, we might suppose, be able to depict himself, to find names to name himself, to describe himself. But the instruments that he uses in all good faith have unexpected repercussions. He offers to give lessons to a banker's children to earn a little money? Immediately, the banker asks around: *who* is Parain? In 1920, that means: was he in the war? And as what? What will Parain's answer be? That he served as a private? This is the truth. But what truth? It is, without a doubt, a social truth that has its place in a system of files, notes and signs. But Parain is also an ex-student of the *grandes écoles* and has the *agrégation*: as such, he *should have been* an officer. 'In saying "private soldier", I am saying for the worker a pal, for the banker a suspect . . . perhaps a rebel—at any rate a problem and not inspiring immediate trust.'[14] And Parain adds:

> If I said 'private', I would be thinking, a casual attitude at the beginning, an honest lack of desire to command, despite the advantages, because I didn't believe myself capable of it, youthful scruples and also friendships already formed, habits of life, and a sense of trust

---

14 From an unpublished essay of 1923.

> keeping me where I am . . . Will [the banker]
> not think: lack of dignity, love of the common
> herd, lack of patriotism? . . . In telling the truth,
> I deceive him more than if I lie.

Parain will choose, then, to say he was a lieutenant. Not in order to lie, but precisely so as to be understood: 'In saying officer, I am saying: one of your kind whom you can recognize'. By officer, then, he means non-revolutionary—a truth he cannot express at the same time as that other truth—that he was a private. This is the experience of the demobilized soldier, which Parain will later record in *Essai sur la Misère humaine*:

> The image of an object . . . evoked by a word is
> more or less identical for two people, though
> only on condition that they speak the same lan-
> guage, belong to the same class of society and
> the same generation; that is to say, ultimately,
> that it is more or less identical within a norm in
> which the differences between the two persons
> can be regarded as practically negligible.[15]

From this he will derive this moral precept: 'If you do not react towards other people's remarks in terms of norms set socially by your milieu and your period, you do not know how to understand them and interpret them,' and this first generalization: 'Taken in isolation,

---

15 Parain, *Essai sur la Misère humaine*, p. 238.

the sign has no other relation to the object signified than one of designation . . . it is, so to speak, floating . . . it acquires reality only within an ordered system.'[16]

In which system does the word 'private' have a meaning—the banker's or Parain the soldier's? But the point is precisely that Parain the soldier would look in vain for a language that is valid for him. He is alone. For the moment there is only one language, the one that the bankers, the industrialists and the old men behind the lines share with the other inhabitants of the towns and cities. You have to choose either to get by with the existing system or to remain silent. But the person who remains silent in the town becomes 'frantic, half-mad'.

> Reduce yourself to silence, even an inner silence, and you will see how some bodily desires intensify to the point of obsession, and how you lose the notion of the social. You will see how you no longer know how to behave, how you cease to understand and have only your feelings, how you become an idiot in Dostoyevsky's sense. You have separated yourself from collective experience.[17]

Should one lie, then? And what exactly is it to lie? It is to give up on expressing an impossible truth and use words not in order to make oneself understood, but so

---

16 Parain, *Essai sur la Misère humaine*, p. 205.
17 Parain, *Essai sur la Misère humaine*, p. 217.

as to be accepted, to 'be loved'. Parain, the most honest of thinkers, the one who indulges least in fine words, is also the one with the greatest indulgence for lying. Or, rather, it seems to him that there are no lies: it would be too much to hope that everyone could lie. That would mean that words have rigorous meanings, that you can put them together to express a precise truth or prefer deliberately to turn your back on that truth. To lie would be to know the truth and reject it, in the same way as doing Evil is rejecting Good. But one can no more lie in Parain's world than one can do evil in Claudel's. For precisely the opposite reasons: for Claudel, the Good is Being. For Parain, Being is imprecise; it floats. I cannot reject the True, because the True is indeterminate: 'Communication is imperfect, not only because thought doesn't wholly contain the individual that it expresses, but also because no word, sentence or work has a necessary meaning without there being a need to interpret it.'[18] Given that state of affairs, in which I perhaps tell an untruth when I want to be truthful, can I be sure of telling an untruth when I mean to lie? We know of those mental patients suffering from the 'psychosis of influence', who complain that their 'thought is being stolen' or, in other words, that their thought is being deflected from its original meaning before it reaches its conclusion. They are not so mad and this is something that befalls every one of us: words drink our thought before

18 Parain, *Essai sur la Misère humaine*, p. 226.

we have the time to recognize it; we had a vague intention, we put it clearly into words and now here we are
saying something quite different from what we meant.
There are no liars. There are only oppressed individuals
getting by as best they can with language. Parain never
forgot the story of the banker or other similar stories.
He still remembers it when he speaks, twenty years later,
of his daughter's lies:

> When my daughter tells me she has done her
> homework even though she has not, she doesn't
> do so . . . *with the intention* of misleading me,
> but to indicate to me that she could have done
> it, that she wanted to do it, that she should have
> done it, but that none of that is of any great
> importance. She does so, then, more to get rid
> of someone who is annoying her than to say
> something untrue.[19]

These are, no doubt, the thoughts that were running
through the mind of the poor demobbed soldier, half-
liar, half-mute, part Myshkin,[20] part Julien Sorel, when
he came away from seeing his banker. As he did so, language, a product of towns and cities, of the 'home front',
came to be seen by him as a privilege of the rich. Parain
borrowed it, but it belonged to others—to the bankers,
generals and prelates and, indeed, to all those who

19 Parain, *Recherches sur le langage*, p. 170.
20 See '*The Outsider* Explained', p. 182, NOTE 15.

handled it with insouciance and consummate, indolent artistry, sure of their ability to be understood by their peers and to impose their words on their underlings. He had the right to use it, but only in the sense—and within the limits—prescribed by the powers that be. With words, the bankers and industrialists wormed their way into him and stole his most secret thoughts, diverting them to their advantage. Language became the most insinuating of instruments of oppression. Worse still, it became the characteristic medium and essential tool of the unproductive, parasitic class of intermediaries. He didn't make this discovery by chance: at the front, as in the fields, Parain had encountered the world of work, for war is hard industrial and agricultural work. He had returned to the peacetime world the way the peasant returns to the village or the miner, after his day's work, comes back to the surface of the earth. He was back in the world of ceremony and good manners, the world of intermediaries in which man is no longer dealing with the soil or the seam or the explosive shell, but with man. Language became an intermediary between man and his desire, between man and his work, in the same way as there are intermediaries between the producer and the consumer. Between man and himself: if I name what I am, I allow myself to be defined within a particular social order and become complicit with it. Yet I cannot be silent. What, then, am I to become?

At about the same time, our age embarked on an adventure that it is still pursuing. And things moved faster than words. Language has its inertia, as has confidence. We know that in periods of inflation prices remain stable for a time while the currency falls: it is the same with words. This produced a new discrepancy from which everyone was to suffer, bankers and war veterans alike. Words chased vainly after their objects, but they had fallen too far behind. What, for example, did 'peace' mean? The Japanese were advancing with guns and tanks into the heart of China; yet they were at peace with the Chinese, since war was not declared. The Japanese and the Russians were fighting on the Manchurian front, yet peace was preserved, since the Japanese ambassador remained in Moscow and the Soviet ambassador in Tokyo. And if two countries are at war and a third keeps out of the operations, can I say it is at peace? Yes, if it remains neutral. But what is neutrality? If it supplies one of the warring parties, is it neutral? If it suffers blockade, is it neutral? Is armed neutrality still neutrality? And what of pre-belligerence? Or intervention? And if we stop defining war as armed conflict, shall we say *the inter-war period* was wartime or peacetime? Everyone is entitled to their own opinion. Blockades, industrial rivalries, class struggles—aren't these enough for us to speak of war? Yet can I not legitimately look back nostalgically to the peacetime of '39? There are people who say that, since 1914, there has been no end to war—and they provide evidence. But others also prove that the war dates from September 1939. So was there a period of peace between two wars or one single war? Who knows? Perhaps there was a single period of peace? Who will decide? I am put in mind here of the uncertainties of biology, whose terms were devised to designate clearly defined species and which suddenly discovered the continuity of living forms. Should we leave words to rot where they stand? 'Our age,' writes Camus, commenting on Parain, 'seems in need of a dictionary.' But Parain would reply that a dictionary presupposes a degree of discontinuity and of stability of meanings; it is, therefore, impossible to establish one today.

> In an age which, like ours, is one of deep social transformations, in which social values disappear without having been replaced yet by others and, by analogy, in any age, since there is no moment that is not undergoing transformation at a greater or lesser rate, no one can know precisely what other people's words mean—nor even their own.[21]

It is at this point, when all is lost, that Parain believes he has found a solution *in extremis*. There are people who have given up trying to understand the world and merely want to change it. Marx writes:

> The question whether objective truth can be attributed to human thinking is not a question of theory but is a practical question. Man must prove the truth, i.e. the reality and power, the

---

21 Parain, *Essai sur la misère humaine*, p. 206.

this-sidedness of his thinking in practice . . . The philosophers have only *interpreted* the world, in various ways; the point is to *change* it.[22]

Wasn't this what Parain was after when, returning from the war, he wrote:

> Not being able to convey exactness, because I do not have the time (and even if I had, where would I find the talent to give an exhaustive chronological description of myself?), not being able to confront someone with the entirety of my personality, with everything in the still effective past and in my intentions that determines it . . . , being a particular human being—that is to say, different from anyone else and incapable by nature of defining within me what might be communicable with precision or, in other words, what in me is identical to something in everyone—I chose to express myself in a role. Giving up on making myself known, I am trying to make myself loved.'[23]

The man who gives up in this way on using words as instruments of knowledge is very close to accepting, out of despair, an anti-rationalist theory of language. That

---

22 This passage, from Marx's 'Theses on Feuerbach', is cited by Parain, *Recherches sur le langage*, p. 121. For the original text, see Karl Marx, *Early Writings* (Harmondsworth: Penguin, 1975), pp. 421–3. [Trans.]

23 Unpublished essay of 1922.

theory existed. And it was more than just a theory; it was a practice:

> Lenin did not believe in a universal value of reason and language; he did not believe in exact communication through language. Life in his view took place below and beyond language: watchwords for him were mere forms given body by activity and given life by personality—if not in individual, then at least in collective terms.[24]

With Lenin, words become watchwords, slogans. It would be pointless to hope for them to have pre-established meanings; they have only the meaning you want to give them; their value is strictly historical and practical. They are the words of the leader, of the dominant class. They are true if they are confirmed or, in other words, if they are obeyed and have consequences. This activist conception of language will represent the great temptation for Parain. When you are battling against a closed door, there comes a point when the desire to break it down gets the better of you. Parain's adherence to the activist doctrine appears to be as much a product of anger as of resignation. To him, the word remains an intermediary, but its function is now clearer: it interposes itself between the desire and its realization. 'What guides man at every moment, what musters him and orders him

---

24 Parain, *Essai sur la misère humaine*, p. 208.

is what he says of himself, of his needs, his desires and his means. These are his watchwords.'[25] This is to recognize a primacy of desire and affectivity. Language is an instrument of realization. With this, reason is reduced to a more modest role.

> Reason is nothing but intelligence, which is itself nothing but the power to build a system of signs to be tested, that is to say the power to frame a hypothesis . . . Reason . . . is the endeavour man pursues . . . to present his desires with an exact, effective means of satisfaction . . . Its subservient role is very precise . . . The desires need to control it frequently, the way one takes an idling workman to task.[26]

With this, the scandal of language becomes clearer: if there is pressure to force Parain to adopt the language of the banker, that is because the banker is in command. For a poor demobbed soldier, the point is neither to strive to understand a language that is not made for him—which would lead him into servitude—nor to invent for himself a system of signs that is valid for him alone—which would lead him straight to madness. He has to find a community of the oppressed that are eager to take power and impose their language, a language forged in the silent solidarity of work and suffering.

---

25 Parain, *Essai sur la misère humaine*, p. 169.
26 Parain, *Essai sur la misère humaine*, p. 167.

Parain can now say, modifying Marx's thesis slightly, 'We do not wish to understand words, we wish to change them.' But if it comes to re-inventing a language, you have to opt for a rigorous, precise one; the wobble in the handle or the 'play' in the gears has to be eliminated. For the order to be obeyed, it has to be understood down to its last details. And conversely, to understand is to act. You have to tighten the drive belts and the screws. Since you cannot be silent—that is to say, accede directly and immediately to being—you have at least to control the intermediaries strictly. Parain admits that his youth was buffeted between two dreams:

> Symbols lead us to believe that by eliminating all transmissions we can be said to be eliminating all hitches and to believe too, conversely, that by perfecting that whole machinery, the mechanisms would function smoothly and accidents would become impossible.[27]

When that first dream, that of the 'idiot', the man on leave wandering around the crowded streets, of the 'frantic, half-mad' demobilized soldier, turned out to be unattainable, Parain threw himself body and soul into the other one, the dream of an authoritarian community of work, in which language is expressly reduced to its subordinate role as intermediary between desire and action, between the leaders and their men, in which

---

27 Parain, *Retour à la France*, p. 186.

everyone understands because everyone obeys, in which the elimination of social barriers also eliminates the 'play' in the gears:

> Thus, after having already experienced an already rigorous social order—war—but one that had still seemed to me to admit of many exceptions and privileges since its mystique was too fragile to gain total sway over us, I came to conceive and desire an even more rigorous social order, the most rigorous that could be achieved.[28]

We have reached the extreme point of Parain's journey. He went no further and the rest is a return. Up to this point, he has merely developed the consequences of his original intuition. Here he is now, adhering ultimately to a pragmatic, relativistic authoritarianism, in which the words 'love' and 'hope' would be given distinct, controlled meanings, as in the case of mathematical symbols. He will come to recognize this revolutionary impulse as a cunning attempt to destroy language:

> If language derives its meaning only from the operations it designates and if it is these operations that constitute the object of our thought, not essences and their naming, then it must ultimately appear useless and even dangerous: useless because we accept that our thoughts all conform to the same pattern of action, which

---

28 Parain, *Retour à la France*, p. 182.

commands us of itself, without language playing
a decisive role and that they develop spontaneously in parallel, and hence harmonious,
directions; dangerous because it then serves
only to provide pretexts for the negligence and
ill-will of the inferiors, who discuss instead of
obeying.[29]

And so Parain, despite having abandoned the pursuit of
what I shall term 'infra-silence', that silence that may be
said to coincide with some sort of 'state of nature' and
to *precede* language, has still not given up on the project
of falling silent. The silence he comes to at this point
extends over the whole domain of language; it is identical with language itself; it is abuzz with murmurs, orders
and solicitations. It is obtained in this instance not by
the impossible destruction of words, but by their radical
*devaluation*. He will later say, passing judgement on his
own endeavour,

Bolshevism was at that point an absolutely
anti-rationalist attitude that completed the
ideological destruction of the individual by a
destruction, carried to the point of heroism, of
the word that did not end in total sacrifice.[30]

29 Parain, *Recherches sur le langage*, p. 119.

30 Sartre provides no source for this quotation. [Trans.]

He was not alone in pursuing these desperate endeavours. In these magnificent post-war years, there were many other young people in revolt against the human condition and, in particular, against the language that expressed it. The obsession with intuitive knowledge or, in other words, with a knowledge without intermediaries, which, as we have seen, first motivated Parain, was initially a driving force of Surrealism, as was that profound distrust of discourse Paulhan has dubbed 'terrorism'. But since one has, in the end to speak, since, whatever one does, the word intercalates itself between the intuition and its object, our terrorists were ejected, like Parain himself, from silence and, throughout the postwar period, we can see an attempt to destroy words with words going on—and an attempt to destroy painting with painting, and art with art. There can be no doubt that this Surrealist destruction should be subjected to existential analysis. We need to know, in fact, what it means to *destroy*. But it is certain that this destruction limited itself, as in Parain's case, to the Word. This is proved to a great extent by Max Ernst's famous definition, 'Surrealism is the encounter, on a dissecting table, between a sewing-machine and an umbrella.'[31] And, indeed, just try to *effect* that encounter. There is nothing in it to stimulate the mind: an umbrella, a sewing-machine and a dissecting table are sad, neutral objects, instruments of human misery that in no sense

---

31 Ernst is following Lautréamont.

clash; they merely form a little reasonable, resigned pile of objects that smack of hospitals and wage labour. It is the words that clash, not the things—the words with their sonority and their repercussions. And this leads on to automatic writing and its subsequent variants, efforts made by *talkers* to set up destructive short-circuits between terms. 'Poetry,' said Léon-Paul Fargue, 'is words burning up.' But he was happy merely to see them sizzle; the Surrealist wants to turn them to ashes. And Bataille will define poetry as 'a holocaust of words' in the same way that Parain defined Bolshevism as 'a destruction of the word'. The last on the list, M. Blanchot, reveals the secret of this endeavour, when he explains that the writer must speak *in order to* say *nothing*. If words annihilate each other, if they crumble into dust, won't a silent reality at last emerge behind them? The hesitation evident here is significant; it is Parain's own hesitation: is this suddenly emergent reality waiting for us, unnamed, behind the words or is it, in fact, *our* creation? If I speak, as Bataille does, of a 'butter horse', I destroy the word 'horse' and the word 'butter', but there is something there—the butter horse. What is it? A *nothing*, obviously. But a nothing I create or one that I disclose? The Surrealist makes no choice between these two contradictory hypotheses and, from his point of view, the choice may be unimportant: whether there is some secret underside to things or whether I create that underside, I am nonetheless an absolute, and the bonfire of words is an absolute event. Hence the Surrealists' flirtation with

Bolshevism: they saw it as an effort, on the part of man, to forge his destiny in absolute terms. It is in this respect that they resemble the Parain of 1925, for does he not write:

> Words must be replaced by a more direct, more effective mode of action, by an immediate mode of action that occurs without intermediaries and abandons nothing of the anxiety from which it issues.[32]

This is because he, like the Surrealists, is driven by the mighty metaphysical pride that was the spirit of the post-war years. By following him, we have arrived at the limit point of the human condition, at that point of tension where the human being attempts to see himself as though he were an inhuman witness to himself. After 1930, the rising generation will register the failure of this endeavour, though some survivors, such as Leiris and Aragon, will go on in their various ways to evaluate it. Let us now follow Parain on the paths back towards his starting point.

## II. EXPERIENCE

When Parain learned that 'the most rigorous social orders taught history, philosophy and literature', he must have felt a little of the stupour experienced by the

---

32 Sartre provides no source for this quotation from Parain. [Trans.]

Pythagoreans at the incommensurability of the sides of a right-angled triangle. If a society philosophizes, this means there is 'play in the gears' and a place for individual dreams, for each person's fantasy, for questioning and incomprehension. That means, then, ultimately, that there is no perfectly rigorous social order, for Parain saw philosophy and literature as the absurd dreams of an imperfect language. However, this purely external experience counts for little in my view, since one can still, in the end, decide to perfect the most imperfect of social orders. Will it *never* be rigorous? Or is it just not rigorous *yet*? The facts do not speak for themselves; it is for everyone to decide. Parain's decision seems, rather, to have been dictated to him by a deeper, more inward experience, a self-testing that is similar in more than one respect to what Rauh termed 'moral experience'. Parain the peasant had set out upon the paths of pride, the ways of the town and the proletariat, as a result of a misunderstanding.

It would be easy to show how the communal disciplines to which he had recently subscribed were at odds with his thoroughgoing individualism. And Parain no doubt felt these contradictions from the first day. But these are conflicts that can be resolved, provided the original wellspring of the individualism is the will to power. It is always easy to obey if one can dream of commanding. Parain wants neither to command nor to obey. His individualism is anything but Nietzschean: it is neither the appetite of a captain of industry, nor the avidity of the urban oppressed, obsessed by the silky, ice-cold mirage of the city shops, but, quite simply, the stubborn, humble claim of the small farmer who wants to remain master on his own land. It isn't so much his individualism as the nature of that individualism that helps to separate Parain from his revolutionary friends. It is up on the plateaux that language is burned, on the plateaux that the great edifices of the capitalist order are set on fire. Parain is a man of the valleys. All these destroyers he followed for a short while are possessed, one way or another, by a demiurgic pride. They are all Nietzscheans in believing in the plasticity of human nature. If they burn the old Man, they do so to hasten the coming of a new one. There is Surrealist man, Gidean man and Marxist man, all awaiting us on the horizon. They have at once to be revealed and shaped. In a sense, the future is empty, no one can predict it; in another sense, the future exists more than the present. The frenzied aim of all these destroyers is to construct a world they don't know and that they won't even recognize when they have built it. This is the joy of risk, the joy of not *knowing* what one is doing, the bitter joy of telling oneself one will lead men to the threshold of the promised land, but will oneself remain on the threshold, watching them recede into the distance. These sentiments are wholly alien to Parain. He has no eyes for the future, he doesn't believe in it. If he speaks of it, it is to represent a world that is unravelling, human beings who are going astray. All in all, his theory of language ought to lead him, and did for a moment lead him, to the idea of human plasticity: change words and you will change human beings. But, in reality, nothing is further from his deepest thinking. The image that lies deepest in his memory is that of the natural order. The return of the seasons and the birds, the growth of plants and children, the fixed order of the stars and planets. It is this order that he secretly set against the artificial order of discourse. The beasts of the field are subject to that order and so is man, that speaking beast. We have seen that, in Parain's mind, words interpose themselves between desires and action. The conclusion should be that the word forges the desire. To give these stirrings, torpors and sudden bursts of anger the name 'love' is to yoke them together by force, to impose a destiny on them from the outside. But Parain sees suddenly that he is reluctant to draw that ultimate consequence. If man *were* what language *makes* him, there would be no problem. But Parain maintains a distance between what I am and what I call myself: man *is* something outside of discourse. There is a pre-established human order, the humble, silent order of needs. Take, for instance, what he says of mothers in *Essai sur la Misère humaine*:

> There isn't a woman—even when they don't admit it right away—who doesn't want to have children . . . [C]alculation speaks against it. They will be unhappy; they will be expensive; they may perhaps die . . . the risk is total. Yet . . . their energy is directed elsewhere. For social

experience and historical truth are arguments; they are not their own experience and truth . . . When they reflect, they have something to reflect on and, behind their reflections their existences are committed and their confidence remains; they are creative in their bodies, their muscles and their glands; *they do not flee from struggle for the sake of words, which are cowardly* . . . What has just been said of children could as well be said of anything else: love, honesty, manual labour, sleep, cash payment—all the things that civilization has left behind and is seeking to rediscover . . . In this way, we can compare what the brain declares impossible and the flesh maintains. What emerges is that it is the role of language to register difficulties as they appear . . . whilst the work of human beings in their bodies and their appetite for life is to deny those difficulties beforehand, so as never to lose the courage to confront them. This is the secret of simple people, of those who, above and beyond civilization, have retained the same simplicity; it lies in this stubborn determination of the body to love and to beget children, to transmit one's enthusiasm and one's joy.[33]

There is, then, an order of the body. But, manifestly, that order isn't purely biological. It was produced

33 Parain, *Essai sur la Misère humaine*, p. 64, p. 66, pp. 73–4.

without words, against words; and yet it cannot be blind. Parain knows this well, explaining that we couldn't say, 'I am hungry' without saying something more—and something different from—what we mean. In order that, beyond vague impressions, women can, without naming their desire, know it and pursue its satisfaction entirely securely, there must be something other than the decree of uterine secretions: a design is needed—a plan. I see that plan—which is herself and yet is neither her language nor her thinking nor exactly her body, but a kind of intention and, ultimately, an entelechy— as something like Grace in the most religious sense of the term. And just as the harmonious course of the stars and the ordered succession of the seasons disclosed the designs of the divinity to the Stoic peasant of Latium, so it seems the encounter within us of this pre-established act discloses for the first time to Parain the fact of religion.

How far we are from the radical post-war experiments! For what Parain doesn't say is that this order of the body naturally involves a social extension; the society that is to correspond to it is one that is properly termed 'conservative'. The point now is not to change man, but to take the measures necessary to ensure that this balance of needs is *conserved*. There can be no new man because there is a natural man. Parain will probably not like me comparing him to Rousseau. But, in the end, isn't the peasant who is exposing himself in his 'rugged honesty' to the deceptions of language the noble savage and

Natural man? Beneath this radical pessimism, there is an optimism of simplicity.

But I see immediately the ways Parain differs from Rousseau. For the Protestant, though the return to the state of nature is an impossible undertaking, the individual can at least achieve an equilibrium for himself more or less alone. Parain isn't so sure of himself. And then he bears the Catholic imprint upon him; he lacks Genevan pride. What he writes, in the belief that he is defining man, depicts only himself: 'Man is an animal who needs assurance . . . The whole history of man is his effort to establish and impose upon himself a mediating system of coordinates, to place himself in the hands of mediating powers . . .'[34] 'Man cannot do without mediating powers, as the earth cannot do without sun; everyone needs a task, a fatherland, children, a hope.'[35]

Nothing, then, is further from him than the great stripping-down process to which his comrades of 1925 invited him. Surrealists, Gideans and Communists all surrounded him then, whispering, 'Leave hold!' To leave hold and abandon himself, to abandon all orders, all coordinates and find himself at last alone and naked, a stranger to himself, like Philoctetes after he has surrendered his bow, like Dimitri Karamazov in prison, like the addict who takes drugs for amusement, like the young man who abandons his class, family and home to place himself alone and naked in the hands of the Party. If he gives all, then he will receive a thousand-fold—that is what these sirens murmur to him. And it is, no doubt, a myth. But Parain doesn't leave hold. On the contrary, he clings on tighter, he lashes himself to the mast. Everyone knows the deep-seated resistance that suddenly reveals itself when one is in danger of coming to grief. Everyone knows too the stunned sense of remorse, the unquenched curiosity and the mulish anger that visits those who survive. Parain didn't come to grief. He didn't want to live without limits. The fields in the countryside have their limits. And roads, major and minor, have their marker posts, their milestones. Why would he lose himself? And what did he ask for? A few acres of land, an honourable wife, children, the humble freedom of the craftsman at work or the peasant in the fields—in a word, happiness. Did he need to lose himself to achieve all that? He never really wanted to launch himself into some great endeavour, and who can criticize him for that? He merely wanted a fairer, almost paternal form of organization to assign him a place on the earth and, by defining him within rigorous coordinates, to rid him of the need for security, of the 'worry that threatened to suffocate him'.[36]

> A man needs a *personal* god. When he isn't sleeping or has lost hope, along with confidence in his own strength, when he is defeated, he

---

36 Parain, *Retour à la France*, p. 22.

really has to turn to something stronger than himself for protection, he really has to find some security somewhere.[37]

So worry is there at the outset, for him as it is for everyone. Worry, anxiety—whatever we want to call it. And then came the need to choose. And some chose precisely this anxiety, but Parain chose security. Is he right or wrong? Who could judge him? And then, isn't the choice of anxiety sometimes a way of choosing security? We can only record that he is what he chose. Humble and assured, clinging to a few sad, simple truths, scanning the high plateaux with an impudent modesty and, perhaps, a secret discontent.

But suddenly the reign of the mediating powers returns. And the reign of language, first among the intermediaries. Admittedly, the earth would be better. 'For a peasant, the earth is that intermediary . . . that serves him as a norm both common and objective.'[38] But there are peasants without land as there are kings without kingdoms. And Parain is one of these; he is rootless. In one corner of his mind, there will remain, nostalgically, the totalitarian myth of an accord binding earthly and human powers, much as a tree's roots merge into the earth that feeds them; beneath his grumpy headmaster's air, he will retain the timid, shamefaced naturalism of the Danubian peasant, that other uprooted individual.

---

37 Parain, *Retour à la France*, p. 105.

38 Parain, *Essai sur la Misère humaine*, p. 99.

But when he has to define himself and settle who he is, he will turn back not to the earth, but to language. It is a question of *being*. And for Parain, as for all post-Kantian philosophy, being is synonymous with stability and objectivity. The planet *is* because its paths across the heavens are set, the tree *is* because it grows according to set laws and doesn't move about. But, from the inside, man is as runny as a soft cheese; he *is* not. He will *be* only if he knows himself. And 'to know oneself' here doesn't mean to discover the truth lodged in everyone's heart: there is no heart and no truth, just a monotonous haemorrhage. To know oneself is to wilfully effect a transference of being: I set myself limits, I set up a system of markers and then I suddenly declare that I *am* these limits and these markers. I *am* a private soldier. I *am* French, I *am* a graduate of the École normale who has passed the *agrégation*. This means that I choose to define myself after the fashion of the sociologist: by means of frames. So, Halbwachs would say, this man being shown into this drawing-room is the gynaecologist, a former Paris hospital houseman and a medical officer during the 1914–18 war.[39] Take away the doctor and the medical officer, nothing remains but a bit of dirty water swirling off down a drain. It's language that makes the doctor or the magistrate:[40] 'He is asked to express what man has

39 Maurice Halbwachs (1877–1944): a student of Bergson and Durkheim, was a close collaborator of Marcel Mauss and the editor of *Annales de Sociologie*. [Trans.]

40 Sartre's reference to magistrates here is a nod towards the saying '*l'habit fait le magistrat*': clothes maketh the man. [Trans.]

that is most intimately impersonal, most intimately similar to others.'[41] The voluntary aspect of language is neglected, namely its transcendence.

This enables us to grasp the dialectical movement that brought Parain back to his starting point. Like everyone, he was convinced at the outset of *being*, deep down, a certain given reality, an individual essence, and he called upon language to formulate that essence. But he realized that he couldn't slip into the socialized forms of speech. He didn't recognize his reflection in the mirror of words. It was at this point that a dual movement revealed a twofold fluidity to him: if he placed himself amid words, in town or city, he saw them melt and flow away, losing their meaning as they passed from one group to another, becoming increasingly abstract, and he set against them the myth of a natural ordering of human needs (love, work, motherhood, etc.). And if words could no longer express these needs, this was precisely because the changeable cannot convey that which stays the same, because made-up terms cannot apply to nature, because the town cannot speak of the countryside. At that point, language seemed to him a destructive force, separating man from himself. But if, deserting words, he wanted to recover his silence, the fixed order of desires he believed he would rediscover immediately vanished, revealing a memoryless, inconsistent fluidity, the shifting, disordered image of the void. Seen from within this fluidity, by contrast,

---

41 Parain, *Recherches sur le langage*, p. 173.

words seemed as fixed as stars: when you are plunged into this little morass we know as love, when you feel tossed about by uncertain emotions, how fine the word 'love' seems, with all the ceremony of affection, desire and jealousy it implies: how you would like to *be* what it *bespeaks*. Parain attempted, then, to hold on simultaneously to these two fleeting entities; this was his expressionist, revolutionary period: language *is* not, it has to be made; the individual *is* not; he has to be named. Only, in the face of these endless, dizzying swirlings, he lost heart, gave up the struggle, clung to what seemed firm. And then, this universal fluidity rendered every solution contradictory: if the individual were to find sufficient coherence and strength in himself to recreate language, he would have to be something fixed and static; in a word, he would have first to be named. And so expressionism is a vicious circle: 'Action [is not] the measure of our language . . . Does it not, rather, presuppose an order that gives rise to it, and hence speech? Can its movement come to it of itself?'[42] And so we see Parain wandering once again from one side to the other: in *Essai sur la Misère humaine* he criticizes language from the standpoint of the order of needs; in *Retour à la France* words are, rather, fixed and restored to their intercessory function; it is we who are boundlessly fluid. But the solution is already forming: an attempt at a modest, positive synthesis and, at the same time, the recourse to God.

---

42 Parain, *Recherches sur le langage*, p. 121.

This solution, which will become clearer in *Recherches*, can be summed up, I believe, in four points:

1. Having a bundle of experiences to put into order, Parain deliberately selects one of them and decides to make it *his* original experience. He constructs his history this way. It is this experience he will define in these terms: 'Man can no more do without language than he can direct it.'

2. It is this experience too that he will cash in through his theory of objectivity. It is the act of naming that divides up the universal fluidity of sensations and stabilizes it into 'things':

> The insect no doubt moves around in its universe of actions and reactions without representing the external world to itself as an object independent of that universe, which thus remains homogeneous. Would we not be equally ignorant if we did not have language? . . . I note the distinctness with which an object detaches itself from me as soon as I have named it. From that moment on, I can no longer deny it the status of object. The philosophers have observed that every perception is constituted by a judgement. But have they stressed sufficiently that it is naming that is the first judgement and that naming is the decisive moment of perception?[43]

---

43 Parain, *Recherches sur le langage*, pp. 22–3.

Words are ideas. This means that man doesn't create ideas, but assembles them. We have been told for a very long time that man isn't God and can create nothing in the universe. He arranges and orders. But the coal, the oil and the marble are there. At least he still had his thoughts, which he produced—so the story went—as a sort of emanation. Parain takes them from him— they are lodged in words. And with that, I am suddenly 'situated in language'.[44] But, as a result, words now become things. Admittedly, Parain tells us that language is 'neither subject nor object, belonging to neither the one nor the other. Subject when I speak, object when I listen to myself . . . and yet distinct from other beings, and distinct, similarly, from the self.' But, despite this caution, he has to recognize that language, as foundation of objectivity, is itself objective: 'Subject when I speak, object when I listen to myself.' But I never speak without listening to myself, as is proved by those deaf mutes who are mute because they are deaf. And how would Parain really accept that words are 'subjects'? How could they confer objectivity if they didn't already possess it? If words seem subjects when I speak, this is because I slip myself into my words; in this sense, the hammer or the spoon are subjects too when I use them and they aren't distinct from my action. And objects the moment after- wards, when I have put them back on the table and am contemplating them. So, having rejected the *chosisme* of

---

44 Parain, *Recherches sur le langage*, p. 183.

perception and reduced the sun, walls and tables to fleeting, subjective arrangements of sensations, Parain deliberately accepts a *chosisme* of language. The word is that strange being: an idea-thing. It has both the impenetrability of the thing and the transparency of the idea, the inertia of the thing and the active force of the idea; we can take it as a thing between our fingers and carry it here or there; but it slips away, betrays us, suddenly regains its independence, and arranges itself with other words of its own accord, obeying affinites that escape our control; individual and dated like things, like ideas it never expresses anything but the universal. We stand in the same relation to the word as the sorceror's apprentice to his master's broom: we can set it in motion, but not guide it or stop it. We are, in one sense, entirely responsible, because we speak, but, in another, we are wholly innocent, because we don't know what we are saying. We are as incapable of lying as of telling the truth, since it is words that teach us what we mean by words. And I refer purposely to the sorceror's apprentice here. Didn't Alain say that magic 'is spirit loitering among things'? Parain's language is the reign of magic. Ideas blinded, blocked by matter; matter possessed by spirit and in revolt against spirit. Not Descartes's 'evil daemon', but a topsy-turvy one.

3. However, Parain hasn't resolved to abandon his expressionist attitude entirely. Language is, no doubt, in a sense, that magical, capricious anti-reason that at times puts itself in the service of man and at times escapes him.

It is, no doubt, *the reverse side of an unknown being's reason.* But Parain cannot ignore the historical life of words; he asserts, as in the past, that words change meaning depending on the group using them. How can this objectivity be reconciled with that relativity? Are there fixed, transcendent meanings or is it the social act that gives its meaning to words? Neither. The fact is that words, for him, have open significations in the sense in which Bergson speaks of 'open' societies. Words are both 'germs of being' and promises.

> Any sign is concrete which, in isolation or within its system, ends in complete accomplishment, as is any promise that is scrupulously kept . . . Man must no longer regard his language as a mere notation of facts and laws . . . but as a *de facto* engagement in the life he sustains and re-creates at every moment.[45]

In a way, the meaning of words lies before them, 'to be filled out'. But if they are to be 'filled out', they are like the empty form which the town-hall clerk or hotelier hands us. One part is variable and one part fixed. It is our action that concretizes them, but the abstract pattern and general outlines of that action are given in advance in every word:

> I tell a woman I love her . . . Have I not simply made a promise? Is it not merely understood

---

45 Parain, *Essai sur la Misère humaine*, pp. 238–92.

between us that this word shall have the meaning we shall give it by living together? We are going to recreate it and that is a great undertaking. Has the word been waiting for us to have this meaning we shall give it? And if it is our intention to give it a meaning, then we are going to work for it, not for ourselves. This means it is our master.[46]

This situation has moral consequences that are impossible to assess: if words are promises, if their meanings are to be constructed, then the ambitious pursuit of *truth*, that is to say, of a deeply buried treasure that is to be extracted, loses all meaning. There is nothing anywhere, on earth or beneath it, that awaits us; nothing with which we can compare the sentences we form. But if the outlines of my promise are already registered in words, if words are like impersonal registration forms that I have to fill up with my life, my work, my blood, then the deep, discreet virtue that lay hidden in our love of truth isn't lost; *honesty* isn't lost. With the expressionist 'watchword', honesty gave way to arbitrary powers of invention and of lawless action—in a word, to force. Truth was measured by success and success was merely a matter of chance. By according a powder charge and a potential to words, by permitting them to hypothecate the future, Parain intends to reserve a role in the world for human beings. He also banishes the marvellous,

---

46 Parain, *Recherches sur le langage*, p. 177.

contradictory power to see the absolute in silence—and the crazed inventiveness that tosses words around haphazardly like pebbles. In exchange, he preserves for man the power to establish a human order: commitments, work, fidelity—these are the things restored to us. And it isn't enough just to be honest, once the promise has been made. We have also to be scrupulous in choosing our promises and to promise little so that we can be sure to keep them. There are wild-eyed, drunken, outlandish words we must be careful to shun. And there are also simple words, such as work, love and family. Parain retained his trust in these and his affection for them even at the height of his crisis. They are human-scale words. It is by them that I should allow myself to be defined, it being understood that that definition isn't the consecration of a factual state, but the announcement of a new duty. If I keep my promises, if I 'fulfil' my commitments, if, having asserted that I love, I carry that undertaking through, then I *shall be* what I *say*.

> The identity of man and of his expression through language . . . is not given at birth. It is the work of the individual who, in achieving it, cannot do without the contribution of society. Much as a man may believe naively in it in his mature years, an adolescent is nonetheless forced to deny it . . . That identity is our task, our need for honesty. It is the happiness and faith we arrive at, but only after long meanderings.

When we express ourselves, we always say more than we want to, because we believe we are expressing something individual and we are saying something universal:

> I'm hungry. I am the one saying 'I'm hungry', but I am not the one who is heard. Between these two moments of my speech, I have disappeared. As soon as I pronounced the words, all that remains of me is the man who is hungry and this man belongs to everyone . . . I have entered the ranks of the impersonal or, in other words, entered on the path of the universal.[47]

Since to speak, however, is to commit oneself, the sense of this morality is clear: as in Kant's system, the aim is to achieve the universal with one's own flesh. But the universal isn't given at the outset, as in *The Critique of Practical Reason*, nor is it the universal that first defines man. I am 'situated' in language, I cannot remain silent; by speaking, I throw myself into this unknown, alien order and I suddenly become responsible for it: I have to *become* universal. To bring into being, with humility and caution, and by means of my own flesh, the universality into which I first threw myself heedlessly—this is the only possibility open to me, the only command I must obey. I have said that I love; the promise is made. I now have to make sacrifices so that the word 'love' assumes meaning through me, so that there is love on Earth. As reward, at the end of this long undertaking, it will fall

47 Parain, *Recherches sur le langage*, p. 172.

to my lot to be *the one who loves* or, in other words, to deserve the name I have given myself. To distrust words and their magical powers; to cling only to some of them, the simplest and most familiar; to speak little; to name things cautiously; to say nothing of myself that I'm not sure I can uphold; to apply myself my whole life long to keeping my promises—this is what Parain's morality offers me. It will seem austere and, so to speak, fearful: he is quite aware of this. The fact is that it occupies a place between an original disquiet and a terminal sense of resignation. It has always been Parain's concern to 'preserve the initial disquiet';[48] it is his conviction that 'man achieves fulfilment with a certain resignation.'[49] It will prove easy to recognize the successive forms of this troubled soul: this perpetual oscillation between the individual and the universal, the historical and the eternal; these perpetual disappointments that suddenly lead us to discover the universal in the heart of the individual and, conversely, reveal the ruse and illusoriness of history to those who believe themselves ensconced in the bosom of the eternal; this contradictory, harrowing wish for a rigorous social order that will nonetheless preserve the dignity of the individual and, lastly, this resigned affirmation that the individual finds accomplishment in the sacrifice in which he destroys himself so that the universal may exist: what is this but that desperate dialectic Hegel laid before us in the Unhappy Consciousness? I am as

48 Parain, *Retour à la France*, p. 23.

49 Parain, *Essai sur la Misère humaine*, p. 123.

nothing when confronted with the compact immobility of words. The point is *to be*. But who will first decide on the meaning of being? Everyone. And everyone will choose himself precisely insofar as he will have made his choice of the nature and meaning of being in general. For Parain, *to be* means fixity, dense fullness, universality. This is the ideal which, from the outset and of his own free choice, he assigned to his existence. But how can the nothingness *be*?

4. We have abandoned everything; we confine our ambition to adapting ourselves progressively to words we have not made. Yet this resignation cannot save us. If words move around, then it is all up with this equilibrium we have acquired with such difficulty. And they do move around. There are quakings of words more dangerous than earthquakes. We are pitched, then, into a universal changeability, since we hook up the restless, living slippages of our individual lives to the slower, more massive slippages of language. From this peril there is only one relief: God. If words come from society, then they are born and die with it and we are their dupes. Happily, 'the arguments ordinarily employed to prove that language cannot have been invented by man are irrefutable.'[50] If it doesn't come from man, then it comes from God:

> Man can no more do without language than he
> can direct it. He can only accord it his trust,

---

50 Parain, *Recherches sur le langage*, p. 175.

attempting, through his resources as a human being and the seriousness of his individual experience, not to abuse it. This law of our thought is the best proof of the existence of God, parallel to all the proofs the theologians have, by turns, advanced, but situated in a narrower domain and perhaps, as a result, more impregnable.[51]

Parain doesn't formulate this proof. Perhaps he is saving it for another book. We can glimpse it nonetheless. In it God appears as both the author and the guarantor of language. He is its author: that is to say, the order that shows through, despite everything, in discourse cannot come from man. In this regard, the proof is akin to the physico-theological argument: it is the order seen in the course of words or in the course of the stars that compels us to deduce the existence of some transcendent purpose. But since, in another sense, that order is postulated more than perceived, since it is a question, above all, of rescuing man from despair by letting him hope for a hidden fixity in the shifting life of words, it may seem too that we have here the so-called moral proof, which deduces the existence of God from the great need we have of Him. It is, in fact, both moral and teleological. Both demand and entreaty at one and the same time. Descartes had limited his ambitions to thinking in clear, distinct ideas; and yet there had to be some guarantor of those ideas. In his work, God appears, then, as

51 Parain, *Retour à la France,* p. 16.

a necessary function. Similarly for Parain, who confines himself to thinking in simple words, to 'making language serve only ends for which its inexactitude presents the least danger,' something must stand surety for these simple words. Not for their truth, since that is still to be made and it is up to us to make it. Nor for their absolute fixity, since they live and die. But rather for a certain stability preserved in the heart of their very mobility. Hegel says somewhere of law that it is the still image of movement: and it is laws that Parain demands of God. It matters little that everything changes, so long as words, the germs of being, have a regulated course to them; so long as there is somewhere a still, silent image of their fluidity. And it has to be that way or else everything will sink into absurdity: things, which don't exist if they aren't named; speech, which will crumble away randomly; and our human condition, since 'we are not beings of silence, but logical creatures.' And just as there is a God for Descartes, because we cannot be mistaken when our will, in spite of itself, is induced to pass an opinion, so there is a God for Parain because we are animals whose main function is to speak.

A strange God, indeed, closer to Kafka's and Kierkegaard's than to the god of Saint Thomas Aquinas. He suffers from a thoroughly modern impotence. The messages he sends to men are scrambled—or, rather, they reach us the wrong way round. Starting out from the bosom of silence and from the unity of a thought governing matter, we receive them as a plurality of noises and it is matter that has subjugated the meanings in them to itself. This God doesn't speak to man, he suggests His silence to him by means of sounds and words. He reminds me of Kafka's emperors, who are omnipotent and yet incapable of communicating with their subjects. Moreover, God too is a word; God is *also* a word. As such, as promise and germ of being, 'God must be . . . applied in terms of the demand that language carries within it and conveys to us.'[52] This perhaps is Parain's theology at its clearest: there is the *word* of God, which suggests to us and at the same time conceals from us the *fact* of God. And we have honestly, by faith and works, to re-create the meaning of that word. Thus, having started out from silence, Parain returns to silence. But it isn't the same silence. His starting point was an infra-silence, a violent mutism of the moment that drove holes in language:

> When I take a walk, there are times when I do not speak. Do not speak to myself, I mean. There are times when, as I look at the mist over the Seine, suddenly timorous, I am struck by the discovery in the sky of something like a policeman's uniform, a jovial fellow or a beautiful woman. Such moments of emotion constitute the only circumstances in which we feel ourselves existing.[53]

---

52 Parain, *Retour à la France*, p. 17.
53 Unpublished manuscript, 1923.

But he understood that this silence had meaning only through the language that names and underpins it.[54] Since words are the basis of objectivity, then if I discover a policeman's uniform or a jovial fellow in the sky, this is because I have at my disposal, in the background, the words 'fellow', 'uniform', 'policeman' and 'jovial'. To be silent is to understand certain implied words; that is all there is to it. Yet the love of silence in Parain is such that he discovers another silence, an ultra-silence, that gathers to itself and runs through the whole of language, in the same way as the Heideggerian nothingness embraces the world or non-knowledge in Blanchot and Bataille envelops knowledge and underpins it. This is merely one of those many surprises that *totalization* keeps in store for us. To contest is, in fact, to totalize. The totality of knowledge is non-knowledge because it appears to a point of view that transcends knowledge. And the totality of language is silence, since one has to be situated in the midst of language to speak. Except that, in the case that concerns us here, totalization is impossible *for man*, since it would be achieved through words. And Parain's silence is merely a great optimistic myth—a myth which he has, if I am not mistaken, now entirely left behind.[55]

---

54 Compare what Bataille says of the *word* silence in *Inner Experience*. [J.-P. S.] See Georges Bataille, *Inner Experience* (Albany: State University of New York Press, 1988), p. 16. [Trans.]

55 He was already tempted by this equation of linguistic totality with silence when discussing Tolstoy's last works with me. These could be equated, he told me, with an 'old man's great silence'. A writer is God

Shall I present a critique of these arguments? I have known Parain for ten years. I have often held discussions with him. I have watched each of the moves made by his honest, rigorous thinking and have often admired his knowledge and the efficacy of his dialectic. To avoid misunderstanding, I shall forewarn the reader, then, that my objections seem to me like a stage in a long, friendly dialogue we have been conducting over many years. He will no doubt respond to my criticism another day, and I shall make other objections to which he will, further, respond. In the meanwhile, his thinking will have followed its course. He will have changed his position and probably I will too. We shall have moved closer together or farther apart; another Parain and another Sartre will carry on the discussion. But since the function of the critic is to criticize—that is to say, to commit himself for or against and to situate himself as he situates his object, I shall say quite bluntly that I accept the greater part of Parain's analyses: I merely contest their scope and their place. What is at issue between us, as has so often been the case in the history of philosophy, is the question of the beginning. Perhaps Parain will be criticized for not starting out from the psychology of the speaking human being. But that isn't my view. Being enough of a Comtian to be deeply mistrustful of psychology, Parain

insofar as he creates his language; and we can totalize his words and speak of the language of Plato or of Shakespeare. As a result, it is beyond his words that he discloses himself and his work can be equated with silence. At this point we are back with Blanchot.

on no account wishes to get into analyses of those 'verbal images' or 'verbo-motor' processes with which the psychologists lethally assailed us in the early years of the twentieth century. He is right: if there are wordless thoughts, as the subjects of Messer and Bühler discovered within themselves around 1905, what concern is that to us? For it would have to be proved that these wordless thoughts aren't framed, limited or conditioned by the whole of language. And the empirical transition from idea to word may very well be described, but what does it teach us? We would have to be sure that the idea isn't simply the dawning of a word. Parain boasts of reconstructing the whole of a man with needs and with words. And if we are talking of the empirical man that psychology claims to grasp, perhaps he isn't wrong. The sociologists argued that the physiological and social facts were enough to make up the human order. We shall perhaps grant them that: it all depends on the definition of the social and the physiological. But is there no other beginning than introspective psychology?

Someone is talking to me. And now the word 'hail' strikes my ears. We have here something precisely located in time and space—in a word, an individual event. Looked at strictly, it isn't *the* word hail that I hear; it's a certain highly particular sound, pronounced in a gentle or husky voice, swept away in a whirlwind, amid light that penetrates it, odours impregnating it and a sadness or gaiety colouring it. Three hours pass and now I am myself pronouncing the word 'hail'. Can we say that I hear myself? Not entirely, since, if you record my voice, I won't recognize it. What we have at this point is a quasi-hearing, which we needn't describe here. And if the word I am *chewing on*, the word that fills my mouth with its substance, resembles the one I heard not so long ago, it does so only insofar as both are individual events. Let us take another individual event: I'm looking at a page in a book, a page glazed by the light of a cold sun; a mouldy cellary smell rises from the page to my nose and, among so many singularities, I see some singular strokes traced on a line: 'hail'. Now I ask Parain, where is the *word* 'hail'? Where is that timeless, dimensionless reality that is, at one and the same time, on the page of the book, in the vibration of the air and in that moist mouthful I taste and which resists absorption by any of these singular phenomena. Where is *this* word, which *was not* either yesterday or the day before yesterday, which *is not* today and *will not be* tomorrow, but which manifests itself yesterday, today and tomorrow, in such a way that each time I hear it, I grasp the auditory phenomenon as one of its incarnations and not as an absolute event? In a word, if language is the ground of objectivity, what is it that grounds the objectivity of language? I see this cockchafer grub and, according to Parain, I need the words 'cockchafer grub' to confer a certain permanency on it, to give it a future, a past, qualities and relations with the other objects in the world. But when I open this book on atmospheric phenomena, I see these little black, spidery marks that make up the word 'hail' in precisely the same way as I see the cockchafer bug. If it's true that this latter, unless it is named, is merely a labile grouping of sensations, then the former cannot exist any differently. Do we, then, need a word to name the word 'hail'? But who will name this word in its turn? We find ourselves, curiously, in an infinite regress; this means that the simple act of naming—and hence of speaking—has become impossible. This is the Third Man argument which was employed by Aristotle in his day against Plato. It isn't unanswerable when applied to pure Ideas, since Plato referred to it himself with some degree of irony in the *Parmenides*. But this is because ideas have no need of ideas to make themselves understood. They are nothing but the act of pure intellection. By contrast, when I consider a word, I see that it has a body and reveals itself to me through that body, amid a host of other bodies. Whence, then, its privileged character? Shall we say it comes from God or from society? But this is a lazy solution. Or rather, we are at a level here where neither God nor society can play a part.

Let us assume, in fact, that, by some divine grace, the word 'hail' is preserved, endowed with a kind of permanence, and that it is the *same word* that struck me yesterday and strikes me again today. After all, it is the same ink bottle I saw a moment ago and see again now; it is the same desk, the same tree. Well, we must confess, then, that even in this unachievable conjecture, the *external* identity of the word 'hail' would be of no use to me; for, however identical it were physically, I would still have to *recognize* it, that is to say, carve it out and stabilize it in the flow of phenomena, relate it to its appearances from yesterday and the day before yesterday, and establish a synthetic site of identification between these various different moments. What matter, in fact, that this ink bottle is the same outside of me? If I have no memory, I shall say there are ten inkbottles, a hundred or as many as there are appearances of inkbottles. Or, rather, I shan't even say there is an inkbottle; I shall say nothing at all. Similarly, where the word 'hail' is concerned, knowledge and communication are possible only if there is *one* word 'hail'. But even if the word existed in the heart of God, I would have to produce it by the operation termed 'synthesis of identification'.[56] And I now understand that the word wasn't privileged, since I have also to make the table and the tree and the cockchafer bug exist as permanent syntheses of relatively stable properties. It isn't by naming them that I confer objectivity on them, but I cannot name them unless I have already constituted them as independent units or, in other words, unless I objectify both the thing and the word in a single synthetic act that names it. I hope no one will imagine replying with the argument that God maintains the identity of the word *within us*, for if God thinks in me, then I vanish; God alone remains. And

---

56 A reference to Husserl's concept, *Identifikationssynthese*. [Trans.]

Parain surely wouldn't go that far. No, it is I, whether listening or speaking, who constitute the word as one of the elements of my experience. Before discussing language, Parain should have asked himself how experience is possible, since there is an experience of language. He has meditated on Descartes, Leibniz and Hegel: all well and good; but he says nothing of Kant. And this enormous lacuna in the *Recherches* doesn't occur by chance: it indicates quite simply that Parain has erred in the order of his thinking. For, ultimately, if I constitute my experience and the words within that experience, it isn't at the level of language, but at the level of the synthesis of identification that the universal appears. When I say, 'I am hungry', then clearly the word universalizes; but, in order to universalize, it must first be the case that *I* individualize it, that is to say, that I extract the word 'hungry' from the disordered confusion of my current impressions.

But we have to go back even further than this. Parain wasn't averse to reproducing a lamentable analysis of the *cogito* that he found in *The Will to Power*. It is well-known that Nietzsche was no philosopher. But why does Parain, as a professional philosopher, rely on this nonsense? Does he really believe he can get away with it? But it matters little what Descartes *says* of the *cogito.* What counts is that, when I understand a word, it is clearly necessary that I am aware of understanding it. Otherwise, the word and the understanding plunge into darkness. Language, says Parain, interposes itself between me and the knowledge I have of myself, though perhaps on condition that knowledge and language are equated, on condition that the relation I have with myself is made to begin with knowledge. But when I am aware of understanding a word, no word interposes itself between me and myself: the word, the sole word in question is there *before* me as *that which is understood*. And where, indeed, would you put it? In my consciousness? You might just as well put a tree in there or a wall that would cut it off from itself. And yet it has to be understood or else it is mere empty noise. After that, it matters little to me that there is such endless discussion over the 'I' of the cogito: that has to do with syntax, grammar and, perhaps, logic. But the efficacy, the eternal nature of the *cogito* is precisely that it reveals a type of existence defined as presence to oneself without intermediary. Words interpose themselves between my love and me, between my cowardice or my courage and me, but not between my understanding and my consciousness of understanding. For the consciousness of understanding is the law of being of understanding. I shall call this the silence of consciousness. And, with this, we are a long way from that flow of sensory impressions to which Parain wants to reduce us. Yet I know what his reply will be: have it your way on your consciousness, but as soon as you try to *express* what you are, you get bogged down in language. I am still in agreement: only I know what I want to express, because I *am* that thing without any intermediary. Language may resist me, may lead me astray, but I shall be deceived by it only if I allow myself to be so, for I always have the possibility of returning to what I am, to that void, that silence that I am, by which, however, there is a language and there is a world. The *cogito* escapes Parain's clutches, as does the synthesis of identification, as does the universal. And that was the commencement.

The fact remains that the *Other* is there, understanding my words, as he wishes, or able to refuse to understand them. But it seems to me precisely that the Other isn't present enough in Parain's work. He intervenes at times, but I don't know where he comes from. Now, this is also a commencement problem. Which is first, the Other or language? If it is language, the Other vanishes. If the Other is to appear to me only when he is named, then it is words that create the Other, as they create the cockchafer grub or hail. And it is also words that can take him away; I cannot escape solipsism: among the flow of my sensations, the word *Other* carves out a certain whole which it endows with a certain universal meaning. This cannot be a privileged experience. But then I speak wholly alone. The alleged interventions of the Other are merely reactions of my language on my language. If, on the other hand, as soon as I speak, I have the agonizing certainty that words slip beyond my grasp, that, outside of me, they are going to assume unsuspected aspects and unforeseen meanings, isn't it then part of the very structure of language that it is to be understood by a freedom that isn't mine? In a word, isn't it the Other who makes language; isn't it the Other that comes first? Parain grudgingly agrees on this point, since he resorts to that Other—that quintessence of otherness—that is God. But why, then, is God needed here? To explain the origin of language? But there is no problem unless man exists first, alone, naked, silent and complete, and speaks *afterwards*. Then one might, indeed, ask how he took it into his head to speak. But if I exist originally only by and for the Other; if, as soon as I appear, I am thrown before the Other's gaze; and if the Other is a thing as certain to me as I am myself, then I am language, for language is merely existence in the presence of someone else. Take this still, hateful, perspicacious woman staring at me silently, as I come and go in the bedroom. All my gestures are immediately alienated, stolen from me; they form, over there, into a horrible package of which I know nothing. Over there I am clumsy and ridiculous. Over there, in the heat of that stern gaze. I pull myself together and battle against this alien ponderousness that suddenly inhabits me. And I become, over there, too jaunty, too conceited—ridiculous again. Here we have the whole of language: it is this dumb, despairing dialogue. Language is being-for-others. What need do we have of God? The Other—any other—is enough. He comes in and I no longer belong to myself; He interposes Himself between me and myself. Not in the silent privacy of the *cogito*, but between me and everything I am on Earth—happy, unhappy, handsome, ugly, mean or magnanimous: for the Other must play a part before I can be any of those things. But if it is true that to speak is to act under the gaze of the Other, there is every danger that the famous problems of language will merely be a regional instance of the major ontological problem of the existence of others. If the Other doesn't understand me, is that because I am speaking or because he is other? And if language plays me false, is this the product of some malignancy specific to it or is it not, rather, because it is the mere surface of contact between me and the Other. In a word, for there to be a problem of language, the Other must first be given.

Against Parain, then, we must maintain the priority of the *cogito*, of universalizing syntheses,[57] and of immediate experience of the Other. In this way we restore language to its true place. However, if its power is thereby limited from above, it is, as I see it, also limited from below; not only by human reality that names and comprehends, but by the objects that are named.

> When, feeling certain inner disturbances, I declare that I am hungry, I am not conveying my sensations to the people I am speaking to, but merely indicating to them that I want to eat

---

57 I have simplified the problem of the syntheses by presenting it in its Kantian form. Perhaps we should speak of 'passive syntheses' as Husserl does or show that, by temporalizing itself, human reality makes use of already *synthesized* complexes. In any event, the argument remains the same: what holds for language holds also for any object, for language is also an object.

or, rather, that I believe I need to eat. I have thought, in fact, that my unease would be settled if I took some food. In doing so, I have put forward a hypothesis concerning my state. But I may be wrong. Amputees actually feel cold in the leg that has been removed.[58]

The fact is that Parain is still under the influence of nineteenth-century psychology, which admits of purely experienced affective states, to which we attach meanings from the outside, out of habit. Isn't this a little premature? And shouldn't he first have taken a stance on the phenomenological conception of affectivity, which regards each desire as an intentional *Erlebnis*, that is to say, as directly bearing on its object. I knew a young woman suffering from a stomach ulcer. When she had gone a long time without food, she would feel a sharp pain and know at that point that she had to eat. In this case, we are certainly dealing with 'affective states' or 'sensations', as postulated by Parain. Only the young woman didn't say she was hungry. Nor did she think it: she presumed that the pain she suffered would disappear if she fed herself. To be hungry, on the other hand, is to be aware of being hungry; it is to be pitched into the world of hunger, to see loaves or meat lit by a painful gleam in shop windows, to catch oneself dreaming of chicken. 'The doctor,' writes Parain, 'would perhaps reject my diagnosis.' But there is no diagnosis—that is to say,

58 Parain, *Recherches sur le langage*, p. 25.

no groping induction tending to interpret mute data—and the doctor cannot help us here. He may explain to me that I shouldn't eat, that there is something suspicious about this hunger, that it corresponds to a certain bodily state far removed from lack of nourishment. But he cannot deny my desire. What would a joy, a pain or a sexual desire be that needed language to assure them of what they are? Language will doubtless extend their scope dangerously, indicating them to me as 'universal desires' and suggesting lines of conduct that could satisfy them. But a desire that didn't give itself out as desire would be in no way different from indifference or resignation. When I have a headache, I *assume* that an aspirin will ease my pain; but my headache is, in no sense, a desire for aspirin. By contrast, when I desire a woman, my desire doesn't want to be eased, but to be satisfied and I don't need to advance an hypothesis as to how I might satisfy it. The desire is there, for those arms and that bosom; either it is a desire for that particular woman or no desire at all.

But, it will be objected, the external object remains: the tree, the table, this darkness. Here we shall not demur; language forms a constitutive stratum of the thing. But it isn't language that gives it its cohesion, shape or permanence. In this case too, it seems to me that Parain's psychological presuppositions are a little dated. Why speak here of sensations? The sensation was consigned to the lumber room a long time ago; it is a fantasy of psychology; for the moment, it is merely a word. The experiments of *Gestalttheorie* reveal, rather, a formal cohesion of objects, laws of structure, dynamic and static relations that surprise the observer, bewilder him and have no regard for whether they are named or not. At night, a gleaming spot on a bicycle wheel seems to me to describe a cycloid; in daylight, the movement of this same spot seems circular. Words cannot affect this; something quite different is in play. The fly doesn't speak, says Parain, and so 'the sensations of flies remain in a rudimentary state.'[59] I find this rather audacious. What does Parain know of the fly? He asserts what actually needs to be proved. In fact, the Gestaltists' experiments tend to show that the least evolved animals behave according to the perception of *relations*, not in terms of alleged sensations. A chicken, a bee or a chimpanzee interprets the *lightest* colour as a signal, not this or that particular shade of grey or green.[60] Does Parain contest the findings of these experiments? If so, he ought at least to say so. The fact is that his knowledge is that of his generation: either he knows nothing of the German psychologists and philosophers of today or he doesn't understand them. He knows very little of Hegel; he is unaware of Kant's unpublished writings; recent work on aphasia by Gelb and Goldstein has passed him by.

---

59 Parain, *Recherches sur le langage*, p. 22.

60 See Paul Guillaume, *Psychologie de la forme* (Paris: Flammarion, 1937).

As a result, he is, without realizing it, thrashing about among outdated problems. He is drawing conclusions that ensue from the movement in French philosophy that runs from Ribot[61] to Brunschvicg[62] by way of Bergson.[63] He is settling accounts and making a final reckoning. For us, these names are all dead and gone, and our accounts with them were long since painlessly and noiselessly settled: we were schooled differently.

Language is situated between stable, concrete objects that didn't await its appearance to reveal themselves (intentional desires, forms of external perception) and human realities that are eloquent in their very nature and, for that very reason, lie outside speech, for they are in direct contact with each other and thrust against each other without intermediary. As a result, language can lie, deceive, distort and make unwarranted generalizations: the questions it raises are technical, political, aesthetic and moral. On that terrain, Parain's analyses retain their relevance. But there is no metaphysical problem of language. And I see flowing from Parain's pen all the theories that encapsulate the attitudes man has assumed in the modern world in respect of himself and his destiny. I find Descartes and rationalism, Leibniz, Hegel,

---

61 Théodule Ribot (1839–1916): French philosopher and psychologist. [Trans.]

62 See 'A Fundamental Idea of Husserl's Phenemenology: Intentionality', NOTE 1.

63 Henri Bergson (1859–1941): one of the foremost French philosophers of his day. [Trans.]

Nietzsche and pragmatism. But there is a constant source of annoyance here, as it seems to me that Parain does much more than interpret them. In fact, he translates them into his own language. Descartes trusts in clear, distinct ideas and Parain translates this as trusting in words. Nietzsche attempts a *logical* critique of the *cogito* and Parain writes that he 'poses the problem of language perfectly, while *believing that he is posing* only the problem of logic'. Modern pragmatism takes as its watchword, Faust's '*Im Anfang war der Tat*' and Parain translates, 'Action is the measure of our language.' The Platonic *logos* becomes discourse and so on. But isn't this a biased view? Isn't this forcing the truth? Has the Greek term *logos* only one meaning? And can't I have some fun myself *translating* Parain's thought? Can't I say that this man, after despairing of knowledge and reason, after having for a time subscribed—in an age when man was trying to forge a destiny for himself—to a kind of radical pragmatism, has returned, with his contemporaries, to a trust in a transcendent order that can assuage his anxiety? What has language got to do with any of that? And if he translates me, I shall translate his translation: and it will be never-ending. Isn't it better to leave each person to say what he meant to say? 'No, sir,' said André Breton to a commentator on Saint-Pol Roux.[64]

---

64 Saint-Pol Roux (1861–1940): a French Symbolist poet, much of whose work was destroyed when his manor house was burned down by invading German troops in 1940. [Trans.]

'If Saint-Pol Roux had *meant to say* "carafe", that is what he would have said.' Doesn't the same apply to Descartes or Hegel?

It is in our hearts that Parain's books are most deeply resonant. It is when he writes, for example, 'I feel I am responsible for a world I did not create,'[65] that we subscribe to what he says wholeheartedly. Parain is a man for whom man exists. Man, not that ready-made reality human *nature*, but man *in situ*, that being who derives his being from his very limits. We love this resigned, but activistic wisdom, this seriousness, this resolve to look things in the eye, this proud, courageous honesty and, above all, this great charity. Perhaps the theoretical principles underlying his work seem a little old-fashioned to us, but in his morality he is akin to the youngest among us. I am thinking, in particular, of Camus. For him, man's response to the absurdity of his condition doesn't lie in some great Romantic rebellion, but in daily application. To see clearly, keep one's word and do one's job—this is our *true* revolt, since there is no reason why I should be faithful, sincere and brave and it is *for that very reason* that I must show myself to be so. Parain asks nothing more nor less of us. He gives us a glimpse, no doubt, of some divine sanction, but his God is too distant to trouble us. Will the young people of these difficult times be satisfied with this morality or is it

---

65 Parain, *Recherches sur le langage*, p. 183.

merely a necessary stage in the exploration of the limits of the human condition? Are Parain himself and Camus satisfied with it? Parain readily agrees that the preference for scrupulous honesty in the choice of words leads the novelist easily into populism. For the words 'bread', 'factory', 'piece-work', 'plough' and 'school' are more familiar to us than 'love' and 'hatred', 'freedom' or 'destiny'. And yet he detests this grey, spineless, horizonless world. Similarly, Camus seems, as a person, to exceed the confines of his doctrine in every way. What will they do? We shall have to wait and see. What Schlumberger says somewhere of Corneille applies admirably to the post-war world, even though he claims to despise it, as well as to the return that followed it and perhaps to what will follow that return:

> There is no great movement that does not start out from some creation . . . with all the harshness, perfunctoriness and, if you will, artifice such a thing implies; nor is there any movement which,—after living on these new models for varying periods of time—isn't succeeded by the need for a more minute focus, for a 'return to nature' or, in other words, to average models. Alternation between the two disciplines is necessary. What a relief when a humbly truthful work puts the great exalted figures back in their place, those figures that have with time become little more than vacuous marionettes! But what

a burst of energy we see when a decisive affirmation produces a new start in a stagnant age of increasingly meticulous, refined and pedestrian analysis, when a man once again sets about that lofty task, the invention of man.[66]

---

66 Jean Schlumberger, 'Corneille', in *Tableau de la littérature française. XVIIe et XVIIIe siècles. De Corneille à Chénier* (Paris: Gallimard/nrf, 1939).

✳

DENIS DE ROUGEMONT:<br>
*L'AMOUR ET L'OCCIDENT* [1]

*[T]he passionate love which the myth [of Tristan and Iseult] celebrates actually became in the twelfth century—the moment when it first came to be cultivated—a religion in the full sense of the word, and in particularly a historically determinate Christian heresy.* Whereupon it may be inferred . . . that the passion which novels and films have now popularized is nothing else than *a lawless invasion and flowing back* into our lives of a spiritual heresy the key to which we have lost. [2]

This is the thesis Monsieur de Rougemont attempts to demonstrate. I must admit that I was not equally convinced by all his arguments. In particular, the attachment

---

1 Denis de Rougemont, *L'Amour et l'occident* (Paris: Union générale d'éditions, 1939). Translated by Montgomery Belgion as *Love in the Western World* (Princeton: Princeton University Press, 1983 [1956]).

2 De Rougemont, *L'Amour et l'occident,* p. 137 (translation modified).

of the Tristan myth to the Cathar heresy is more asserted than proved. Elsewhere, M. de Rougemont has need, in support of his cause, to show that the Chinese know nothing of passionate love. He asserts, as a consequence, that this is the case and I am only too willing to believe it. But it occurs to me immediately that China has five thousand years of history and enormous, highly diverse populations. I go immediately to the Appendix in which M. de Rougemont justifies his assertions and I see that he bases the whole of his psychology of the Chinese on a short passage from *Désespoirs*, a posthumous anthology of the writings of Leo Ferrero.[3] Is this really serious? But perhaps he has other unstated reasons for not weighing down his treatise with references: let us grant him the Chinese. It will be more difficult to let pass most of his ideas on contemporary literature. On page 233, for example, our author cites Caldwell, Lawrence, Faulkner and Céline, in no particular order, as representatives of a mystic doctrine of life, which is said moreover to lie at the origins of the 'National-Socialist' movement. Faulkner as a representative of a mystic doctrine of life? Caldwell a cousin of the Nazis! One can only advise M. de Rougement to re-read—or to read—*Light in August* and *God's Little Acre*. But this is the danger of panoramic visions of this kind.

Happily, this is not entirely a work of such casual audacity. The insightfulness of the analyses, the subtlety

---

3 Leo Ferrero (1903–33): an Italian writer and dramatist. [Trans.]

and originality of certain comparisons (the chapter on love and war is, in my view, excellent) and the deftness of style are certainly worthy of admiration. But the interest of the book, for me, lies primarily in the fact that it reflects a recent, thoroughgoing freeing of historical method under the threefold influence of psychoanalysis, Marxism and sociology. It is to sociology, it seems to me, that M. de Rougemont owes his intention to treat myth as an object of rigorous study. However, his approach will be that of the historian. That is to say, he will not be concerned to compare primitive mythologies so as to extract their common laws: rather, he selects a particular myth, which can be precisely dated, and follows its individual development. The comparison that comes to mind is with Roger Caillois—not the Caillois who explains the myth of the preying mantis, but the Caillois who studies the formation and development in the nineteenth century of the myth of Paris as *great city*—but I am rather afraid that, being so different from each other, the comparison will annoy both authors. They will, however, agree that they have, at least in this particular case, a single approach to myth as both an expression of general affective reactions and the symbolic product of an individual historical situation. Moreover, this idea of myth is itself a product of the age and has been very much in vogue since Sorel.[4] Wasn't it Bloch who called recently for a myth for the

4 Georges Sorel (1847–1922) argued that myth could play a legitimate mobilizing role in radical social movements. [Trans.]

twentieth century?[5] And didn't Malraux speak, precisely, of the myths of love in the preface he contributed to a translation of D. H. Lawrence? To the point that we may fear—to speak like these authors—that there is today a myth of the myth, which ought itself to be subjected to sociological investigation.

I don't think either that M. de Rougemont would unreservedly admit the influence of dialectical material-ism that I believe I discerned in his book. And I will acknowledge, if he so pleases, that it is not direct: I am not forgetting that our author is a Christian. But, where else, ultimately, does he get the precious idea that there are deep analogies and correspondences between the various superstructures of a civilization? For our author, a society seems to be a signifying totality whose compo-nents, each in their own way, express a single meaning. A Marxist wouldn't disagree. And isn't this idea of a sort of logic specific to each superstructure, which seems both to reflect a basic situation and to develop through human consciousnesses in accordance with objective laws of development, a Marxist conception? At this level, and by supposing an objective development of the mind or, if one prefers, of ideologies, we connect up also with psychoanalysis: 'The myth, that is to say, the uncon-scious . . .' writes M. de Rougemont as a true Freudian; and when he interrogates the troubadours and *trouvères*,

---

5 Jean-Richard Bloch (1884–1947): a French novelist, playwright and critic. [Trans.]

he shows little concern for whether or not they were conscious of the esoteric value of their songs. Societies, like human beings, have their secrets; myths are symbols—like our dreams. Hence this new mission for historians: to psychoanalyse texts.

The most fortunate outcome of these divergent influences is, without doubt, its disposing M. de Rougemont to take a *verstehend* approach to the interpretation of historical phenomena. This use of *Verstehen*, the logic of which Raymond Aron has attempted to trace in his *Introduction to the Philosophy of History*, seems to me to mark a genuine advance in historical studies. I should make clear that we shall not find in M. de Rougemont's work either those causal series that can be established by the sociologist (as, for example, the connection made by Simiand[6] between rising wages and the discovery of goldmines in the nineteenth century), the rational deductions of the classical economist or those mere chronological lists of facts we find too often in Lavisse or Seignobos.[7] Our author is attempting to bring to light relations of understanding that relate to the objective spirit of communities, which we shall define briefly here as the revelation of a certain type of finality immanent in cultural phenomena.

6 François Simian (1873–1935), a student of Durkheim and Bergson, was a French economist and sociologist.

7 Ernest Lavisse (1842–1922): a French historian and, famously, an editor of French official school manuals in his subject; Charles Seignobos (1854–1942): an equally renowned positivist historian. [Trans.]

Thus, passionate love is not a primal datum of the human condition. We may assign a date to its appearance in Western society and we may imagine its total disappearance: 'The enforced practice of eugenics may succeed where all moral doctrines have failed, resulting in the effective disappearance of any . . . need of passion.'[8] This idea is not perhaps as new as it first seems. In his study, 'Prohibition of Incest', Durkheim suggested that our modern concenption of love had its origins in primitive man being forbidden to take a wife from within his own clan. If it had been permitted, he said, incest would have made the sexual act an austere, sacred family rite. But in the writings of M. de Rougemont, who is a Christian, this degree of historicism may be surprising. This is because historicism, if taken to its limits, leads automatically to total relativism. On this path, M. de Rougemont stops at a point that suits him: he asserts, in fact, the absolute of faith. This enables us to grasp the ambiguous nature of Christianity, which is the *historical* revelation of the absolute. There is nothing inherently shocking in this paradox, since human beings are such that they experience eternal truths *in time*. But M. de Rougemont will have to be careful. If he takes advantage of the *historicity* of the 'passionate love' phenomenon to assert its relativity, he prompts us to want to do the same with religion. And if he defends his faith with the contention that the absolute may very well

---

8 De Rougemont, *Love* . . . , p. 291 (translation modified).

appear to us *in time*, then we shall ask in turn: if that is the case, then why couldn't certain essential structures of the human condition realize themselves through determinate historical conditions? What is there to prevent me from supposing that in Greece passionate love was *masked* by paganism, by the religion of the *polis* and by the power of family constraints? Indeed, I believe I have noticed a slight vacillation on this question in our author's thinking. He seems to believe, at times, that passion is the normal outcome of natural Eros and he even goes so far as to speak of the 'perpetual threat that passion and the death instinct present for the whole of society', and at times he calls it 'the oriental temptation of the West'. But, he will no doubt say, this is the same thing, since the Oriental is natural man. Well, not exactly, since M. de Rougemont himself acknowledges that 'these same beliefs have not produced the same effects among the peoples of the East.' This is because they have not, he says, met with the same obstacles: 'Christian marriage, by becoming a sacrament, imposed an unbearable fidelity on natural man . . . He was ready to welcome, under cover of Catholic forms, all the revivals of pagan mysticism that were capable of liberating him.' Right. But this takes us a long way from that 'perpetual threat' which passion poses for every society. Passionate love is, indeed, a debased myth. And M. de Rougemont is curiously close to the psychoanalysts since, like them, he asserts that human affectivity is originally a *tabula rasa*. It is the circumstances of individual or collective history that inscribe their lessons upon it. All this is not very clear. Nor perhaps is it coherent. And the distinction between the natural man and the man of faith, which the author accepts throughout as though it were self-evident, probably requires some explanation. But no matter. Let us take the argument as presented to us and consider its merits.

For my part, I admire its ingenious nature, but I do not believe it at all. It would first have to be proved that literature expresses *mores* exactly. And also that it influences them. M. de Rougemont confines himself to asserting that influence because, he says, 'passion has its source in that surge of the spirit which, moreover, gives rise to language.' This is true. But language and literary expression are not the same thing. To attempt to study a myth solely on the basis of its literary—in other words, its conscious, reflective—forms is like trying to determine the *mores* of a community by looking at its written law. At most, M. de Rougemont has shown that literature creates a fixed representation of passion, something like a label of passion, which may perhaps underlie many an amorous adventure. But we knew that already. We have known it since Stendhal. 'If the word love is spoken between them, I am lost,' says Count Mosca, as he watches the coach carrying la Sanseverina and Fabrice recede into the distance. But does *real* passion, the passion that suddenly forms within a soul, also crystallize in these stereotyped forms? Is it true that without them it would be just a dumb, obtuse sexual desire? Would it not, as a psychological phenomenon, have its own dialectic? And are not its eager, hapless efforts aimed at removing obstacles, rather than constantly giving rise to new ones? This is what ought to have been elucidated. I hear M. de Rougemont telling me that the sexual instinct, when left to itself, is incapable of dialectic. If he is referring to that itching of the loins that nineteenth-century psychology describes as sexuality, then I agree with him. But the question remains whether sexual desire is really an itching of the loins.

It seems to me that M. de Rougemont touches on the real problem when he writes, 'The history of passionate love . . . is . . . the account of the more and more desperate attempts Eros makes to replace *mystical Transcendence* with an emotional intensity.'[9] Here we are then: passionate love, like mysticism, raises the question of transcendence. But the author brings to the examination of the problem the immanentist, subjectivist prejudices of a psychology that has had its day. What if transcendence were precisely the 'existential' structure of the human being? Would there still be a narcissism of love? Would we need a courtly myth to explain passion? M. de Rougemont hasn't speculated on this. And yet these questions are essential. If man is 'transcendent', then he can exist only by transcending

---

9 De Rougemont, *Love* . . . , p. 170 (translation modified). My emphasis. [J.-P. S.]

*himself*, that is to say, by throwing himself out of himself and into the world—what Heidegger calls *Sich-vorweg-sein-bei*. In this case, to love is merely one aspect of transcendence: one loves outside of oneself, beside another; he who loves depends on another to the very heart of his existence. And if M. de Rougemont should find that this word 'love' refers to a sentiment that is already too developed, I shall tell him that sexual desire is, itself, transcendence. One doesn't 'desire' a mere evacuation, like a cow who is going to be milked. Nor even the highly subjective impressions afforded by a fresh contact. One desires a person in her flesh. To desire is to throw oneself into the world, in danger beside the flesh of a woman, in danger in the very flesh of that woman; it is to wish to attain a state of consciousness, through the flesh and *on* the flesh—to attain that 'divine absence' Paul Valéry speaks of. Is anything more required for desire naturally to entail its own contradiction, its haplessness and its dialectic? Doesn't it seek a union which, by its nature, it rejects? Isn't it desire for the freedom of another which, by its essence, eludes it? Lastly, if it is true that man's authentic being is a 'being-for death', any authentic passion must have a taste of ashes about it. If death is present in love, this is not in any sense the fault of love or of any sort of narcissism; it is the fault of death.

Since it makes no attempt to discuss these problems, M. de Rougemont's book seems merely a fine piece of entertainment. But no matter. Read it. It will give you great pleasure. Perhaps you will catch yourself dreaming of what might have happened if, by some miracle, the Cathars had massacred all the Christians (it was, unfortunately, the opposite that happened) and if their religion had continued into our own day. They were decent people.

*

*A NOTE ON SOURCES*

### 'Cartesian Freedom'

Originally published as 'La liberté cartésienne' in *Situations I* (Paris: Gallimard, 1947), pp. 289–308.

First published in English translation in *Critical Essays* (London: Seagull Books, 2010), pp. 498–529.

### 'A Fundamental Idea of Husserl's Phenomenology'

Originally published as 'Une idée fondamentale de la phéno-ménologie de Husserl' in *Situations I* (Paris: Gallimard, 1947), pp. 29–32.

First published in English translation in *Critical Essays* (London: Seagull Books, 2010), pp. 40–46.

### 'There and Back'

Originally published as 'Aller et retour' in *Situations I* (Paris: Gallimard, 1947), pp. 92–112.

First published in English translation in *Critical Essays* (London: Seagull Books, 2010), pp. 294–382.

### 'Denis de Rougemont: *L'Amour et l'occident*'

Originally published as 'Denis de Rougemont: *L'Amour et l'occident*' in *Situations I* (Paris: Gallimard, 1947), pp. 57–64.

First published in English translation in *Critical Essays* (London: Seagull Books, 2010), pp. 92–103.